REFLECTION IN ACTION

To Barry

Reflection in Action

Developing Reflective Practice in Health and Social Services

BAIRBRE REDMOND

ASHGATE

Published by
Ashgate Publishing Limited
Gower House
Croft Road
Aldershot
Hampshire GU11 3HR
England

Ashgate Publishing Company
Suite 420
101 Cherry Street
Burlington, VT 05401-4405
USA

Ashgate website: http://www.ashgate.com

British Library Cataloguing in Publication Data
Redmond, Bairbre
    Reflection in action : developing reflective practice in
    health and social services
    1. Social workers - Attitudes 2. Medical personnel -
    Attitudes 3. Social workers - Attitudes - Research 4. Medical
    personnel - Attitudes - Research 5. Social work education
    6. Medical education 7. Self-knowledge, Theory of 8. Medical
    personnel and patient 9. Physician and patient
    I. Title
    361.3'2

Library of Congress Cataloging-in-Publication Data
Redmond, Bairbre, 1953-
    Reflection in action: developing reflective practice in health and social services / Bairbre Redmond.
        p. cm.
    Includes bibliographical references and index.
    ISBN 0-7546-3356-X (Hbk) ISBN 0-7546-4955-5 (Pbk)
        1. Medicine--Study and teaching. 2. Learning. 3. Active learning. 4. Medical education.
    5. Reflection (Philosophy) 6. Thought and thinking. I. Title.

    R737.R34 2003
    610'.71'1--dc22

                                                                        2003062721
ISBN-10: 0 7546 3356 X (Hbk) 0 7546 4955 5 (Pbk)
ISBN-13: 978-0-7546-3356-3 (Hbk) 978-0-7546-4955-7 (Pbk)

Graphic design: Maeve Kelly

Printed and bound in Great Britain by MPG Books Ltd. Bodmin, Cornwall.

Contents

List of Figures

Preface

When this book was first published in 2004, the concept of reflection and reflective practice was already being introduced on to many professional health and social care courses, particularly in the areas of social work and nursing. Such curriculum developments manifested themselves in different ways, from the ubiquitous learning journal to more thorough exploration of the academic work of the reflective theorists. It was occasionally unclear to students as to whether they were being presented with a new and perplexing practice theory in itself, or just being scrutinised on the motivations behind aspects of their practice. For many of us who had begun to see the considerable gains that could accrue from developing a reflective stance in our practice, the temptation to want to encourage new and developing practitioners to approach their work with, in Dewey's words, 'active, persistent, and careful consideration' (1933: 118), was very strong. What many lecturers and trainers soon learned was that undergoing a personal conscientization was one thing, but creating an educational environment where one's students also could begin to appreciate the subtleties of reflective practice was a great deal more complex and perplexing. This book follows the process of the creation of one such environment.

Since writing this book I have, at times, been asked two interconnected questions – one is to whether the basis of my work is 'reflective' or 'reflexive' and, if the former is the case, whether that reflection is critical reflection. Payne (2005: 35) notes that two important developments in reflective practice that have come into focus in the late 1990s and the early 2000s have been critical thinking and reflexivity. The debate around what differentiates reflectivity from reflexivity is considerable and the two ideas may be perceived as having emerged from different schools of thought. The roots of reflection are in the educational and professional discourse closely associated with the work of Dewey and developed on by Schön, Argyris and Mezirow, a lineage comprehensively explored in this volume. Reflexivity is more closely connected with a constructionist background and Mead (1934) described reflexivity as a turning back of one's experience upon oneself, with the self and the experience being socially constructed (Steier 1991: 2). Reflexivity also has a strong tradition in qualitative research where both the research process itself and the researcher's own position must be open to an on-going process of self-critique and self-appraisal (Koch and Harrington 1998). This approach has many similarities to the action research approach and the use of critical friends adopted in this volume, where both the direction of the research and the position of the researcher are placed under scrutiny. Fook (2002: 43) differentiates between the process of reflecting upon action while the reflexive stance refers more to the ability to appreciate the impact of one's self within the action. While Fook suggests that reflexivity is potentially more complex than reflection, she notes that the reflective process and the reflexive stance are not mutually exclusive and that frequently the reflective process will be underpinned by a reflexive stance. The theory that I have developed in this book proposes that the ability to reflect on one's actions and to appreciate and incorporate the service user's perspective in practice can be seen as a phased capability. Chapters Six and Seven explore this increasingly multifaceted reflective ability, from simple to complex reflection. I would contend that the more complex levels of reflection defined in the later chapter contain all the characteristics of the reflexive stance, particularly the appreciation of the self within the action.

Critical Reflection, Postmodernism and Power

Even before the first publication of this book in 2004, the term 'reflection' had become ubiquitous in much of the professional literature relating to health and social services, being used to describe anything from a passing deliberation on a topic to a fundamental re-assessment not only of a personal stance but also of the discourse within which it existed. Also the terms 'reflection' and 'critical reflection' have often been used interchangeably, without much regard as to what defines the critical nature of a reflective episode. Certainly not all reflection is necessarily critical and to engage in critical reflection individuals must move 'beyond the acquisition of new knowledge and understanding [of] existing assumptions, values and perspectives' (Cranton 1996: 76). The antecedents of critical thought and critical reflection are well documented in Chapter Two of this book, particularly in the overview of the work of Jack Mezirow, Jurgen Haberman and Stephen Brookfield. More recent work has sought to differentiate reflection from critical reflection by focusing on the social and culture contexts in which action occurs. Baldwin (2004: 43) notes that reflection becomes critical when it has the ability to construct and reconstruct practice knowledge in a way that allows a practitioner to recognise and avoid using ineffective or discriminatory approaches with service users.

Some current authors have also linked critical reflection with critical thinking and a postmodern perspective. Morley (2004: 298-299) argues that, in terms of globalization, economies and technologies have left certain groups increasingly marginalized. Morley proposes that critical reflection, informed by postmodernism, can provide us with new processes and strategies to work towards social change to address such inequities. Most notably Fook's (2002) work on critical social work has identified similarities between a critical and a postmodern approach to professional practice in that both recognize interactive and reflective ways of knowing and both recognize the possibilities for personal and social change. Fook (2002: 14) highlights the possibilities in postmodern thinking of re-conceptualizing and valuing the marginalized voices of service users and practitioners, an issue highlighted in this book in the case of service users and of practitioners facing unhelpful or oppressive agency practices.

The service users who are focused upon in this book are parents of people with an intellectual disability. Unlike their children, they are a group not generally considered socially oppressed in the general meaning of the term. Their oppression, however, can be perceived as emanating from the power differential existing between themselves and the health and social service professionals who have, by force of circumstance, become part of their lives. Postmodern thinking offers a number of different interpretations on how we see our world, but it argues that different power structures control these perspectives, making some more legitimate than others. It is only through critical reflection that an understanding of such power differentials can be explored and challenged. Fook (2004: 58) argues that critical reflection involves a deconstruction and reconstruction of different aspects of power including personal, interpersonal, structural, formal and informal aspects. In postmodern terms, this book demonstrates how a group of practitioners can use the classroom to consider how some of these aspects of the power differentials in their relationships with service users impact on the quality of work that they can achieve with these families. Through reflective teaching encounters they deconstruct the relationships they have had with service users and try to reconstruct new, less oppressive approaches and to consider multiple and diverse constructions on their practice.

Critical Reflection and the Learning Organization

An issue of current interest and one that emerges in this book is the impact of agency practices and procedures on the quality of work that individual practitioners can achieve. This is also connected to the effect on an organization when individuals within that organization become more reflective in their own practice. This interlinking between individual learning, the ability of the organization to incorporate that learning and the ability of the organization to become a dynamic learning entity in itself has been a natural development of reflective thinking. Gould (2000) argues that, in professional practice, the concept of learning exists both within the personal experience of the learner and also involves the construction and reconstruction of meanings and world views within organizations. Such a recognition thus connects the concept of the learning organization with the concept of reflective practice (Gould 2004).

One of the issues that emerges in Chapter Eight of this book, and is dealt with in more depth elsewhere (Redmond 2004), relates to the difficulties of practitioners who want to adopt a more reflective approach when this desire is hampered by an organization whose structure is unable or unwilling to support such change. The awareness that organizational structures limit practitioners' ability to become more reflective in their work confirms Schön's assertion (1983) that many organizations tend to resist a professional's attempt to adopt critically reflective practice. Baldwin (2004: 48) sees managerialism, specifically managerialism in social service agencies, as a significant block to both individual learning, critical reflection and organizational learning. While he does not place the blame on individual managers per se, he recommends an exploration of the organizational culture that positions managerial practice in a way that creates such a threat to individual and organizational learning.

Senge talks of the importance of starting, in the learning organization, from the perspective of the individual practitioner and of allowing that personal vision to become the basis of the shared vision of the organization. He warns that when a top-down, organizational vision is imposed 'the result is compliance, never commitment' (Senge 1992: 211). Unfortunately, some practitioners in health and social care areas face the frustration of practicing within organizational constraints that fail to encompass their personal vision or view such perspectives as a threat to organizational stability. When such barriers to organization learning become insurmountable then practitioners may no longer remember that they ever had a vision about their work at all and are in danger of losing what Senge described as their personal mastery, leaving them with little option in how they can practice.

Gould (2000) warns that individual learning is a necessary, but not sufficient condition for organizational learning and that learning cannot be confined to a discrete education event, instead learning must incorporate the complex organizational structures and meaning within which the learner operates. However, after the original research reported on in this publication, a colleague and I returned to this group of professionals to examine the longer-term implications for the group of attending the university for further training. This research (Redmond and McEvoy 2002) revealed that 83 per cent of the professionals with whom I had worked within the reflective teaching model considered that, over two years after the end of the course, they were significantly more confident of being able to introduce change within their organization. While this finding cannot be solely attributed to the respondents' exposure to a reflective teaching environment, it does give some cause for optimism that individual reflective learning may have an impact on the confidence of the learner both to recognize and to contribute to organizational learning.

Development in Reflective Education and Practice across the Professions

This book explores the development of reflection in a number of health and social service professions, primarily social work and nursing, although other professions were also involved in the research. Whereas these professions have continued to develop a strong interest in the development of critical reflection, there have also been recent developments in both interprofessional reflection (Ross, King and Firth 2005) and in reflective work with professionals hitherto not appreciably involved in the reflective sphere. Although still not well represented in the reflective literature, medicine has begun to use reflective teaching approaches, such as critical incident reports, to try and encourage a critically reflective approach in its practitioners (Branch 2005). The importance of the reflective process underlying a number of the expected medical competencies has also been recognized by some of the medical accreditation bodies, such as the Accreditation Council for Graduate Medical Education (ACGME) in the United States of America (Plack and Greenberg 2005). Clouder and Sellars

(2004) note that formalized reflection is embedded in undergraduate programmes for both physiotherapists and for occupational therapists although they conclude that, unlike nursing, a lack of clinical supervision may inhibit the development of critical reflection in graduate practice. Indeed, both Jones (2004) and Karvinen-Niinikoski (2004) highlight the importance of supervision in offering social work practitioners an essential forum not only for reflection on practice, but also on understanding of the organizational networks in which they operate.

Social work, nursing and education have continued to develop practice and research innovations based on reflective ideals both in the area of professional education and in professional practice. Reflective practice is now central to both social work and nursing education and practice. In their review of the literature on reflection in nursing education over a period of almost fifteen years, Cook and Matarasso (2005) found that as a process, reflective learning is a means by which the learner can develop and strengthen skills needed to become a lifelong reflective practitioner with attendant benefits to effective client care. These authors, along with others, have also looked at developing critical reflection for nursing practise through the introduction of problem based learning approaches (Williams 2001) In social work the developments into postmodern thinking have already been noted. Reflection has also been highlighted as a necessary component in the assessment process and Baldwin and Walker (2005) propose an action/reflection model for social work assessment that bears a close similarity to Kemmis and McTaggarts's action research model utilized in this book.

Final Thoughts

It is now well over twenty years since Schön wrote *The Reflective Practitioner*. In doing so he provided a bridge that introduced what had been, up to then, largely educationally based reflective thinking to a much wider group of professions and his work has also done much to produce a new generation of writers in the area of critical reflection. Certainly not all of the professions or the professionals who initially explored the work of Schön and other theorists have developed the concepts into their own professional contexts in the same way. While some professions have continued to advance innovative approaches that encourage the 'reflective turn' in their practitioners, other settings are more limited in their approach to the concept, sometimes viewing reflection as simply another measurable skill that should be required of its practitioners. For example, as more of the work of health and social service practitioners is starting to come under some form of outcome evaluation and measurement, the appearance of 'ability to reflect' as an assessable category on a competency checklist can only be regarded as a retrograde step, lacking any basic comprehension of the concept.

In all the debate about reflective practice, there is one simple and important aspect of reflection that is sometimes in danger of being forgotten. When practitioners critically reflect on what they do and when they reconstruct their practice to more

Reflection in Action

effectively incorporate the perspectives of the service user, then their chances of obtaining a better result, both for themselves and for the service user are enhanced. This is a straightforward and pragmatic premise, but it contains within it the motivation and the reward for reflective practitioners to continue to be reflective. The challenge that lies before those of us who educate practitioners is to help them to experience what reflective practice is like and to encourage them to judge for themselves the value of the approach both for themselves and for the service user. If we can achieve this, then we begin to move them towards Dewey's vision of reflective open-mindedness – that 'active desire to listen to more sides than one; to give heed to facts from whatever source they come; to give full attention to alternative possibilities; to recognize the possibility of error even in the beliefs that are dearest to us' (1933: 29).

> *'Man's mind, once stretched by a new idea, never regains its original dimensions.'*
> Oliver Wendell Holmes

References

Baldwin, M. (2004) 'Critical Reflection: Opportunities and Threats to Professional Learning and Service Development in Social Work Organizations' in N. Gould and M. Baldwin (eds) *Social Work, Critical Reflection and the Learning Organisation*, Aldershot, Ashgate.

Baldwin, N. and Walker, L. (2005) 'Assessment' in R. Adams. L. Dominelli and M. Payne (eds) *Social Work Futures: Crossing Boundaries, Transforming Practice*, Hampshire, Palgrave Macmillan.

Branch, W.T. (2005) 'Use of Critical Incident Reports in Medical Education: A Perspective', *Journal of General Internal Medicine,* vol. 20, no. 11: 1063-1067.

Clouder, L. and Sellars, J. (2004) 'Reflective Practice and Clinical Supervision: an Interprofessional Perspective, *Journal of Advanced Nursing*, vol. 4, no 2: 262-269.

Cooke, M. and Matarasso, B. (2005) 'Promoting Reflection in Mental Health Nursing Practice: A Case Illustration Using Problem-Based Learning', *International Journal of Mental Health Nursing*, vol.14, no. 4: 243-248.

Cranton, P. (1996) *Professional Development as Transformative Learning: New Perspectives for Teachers of Adults*, San Francisco, Jossey Bass.

Dewey, J. (1933) *How We Think*, Chicago, Henry Regnery.

Fook, J. (2002) *Social Work: Critical Theory and Practice*, London, Sage.

Fook, J. (2004) 'Critical Reflection and Organizational Learning and Change' in N. Gould and M. Baldwin (eds) *Social Work, Critical Reflection and the Learning Organisation*, Aldershot, Ashgate.

Gould N. (2000) 'Becoming a Learning Organisation: A Social Work Example', *Social Work Education*, vol. 19, no 6: 585-596.

Gould, N. (2004) 'The Learning Organisation and Reflective Practice – The Emergence of a Concept' in N. Gould and M. Baldwin (eds) *Social Work, Critical Reflection and the Learning Organisation*, Aldershot, Ashgate.

Jones, M. (2004) 'Supervision, Learning and Transformative Practices' in N. Gould and M. Baldwin (eds.) *Social Work, Critical Reflection and the Learning Organisation*, Aldershot, Ashgate.

Karvinen-Niinikoski, S. (2004) 'Social Work Supervision: Contributing to Innovative Knowledge Production and Open Expertise' in N. Gould and M. Baldwin (eds) *Social Work, Critical Reflection and the Learning Organisation*, Aldershot, Ashgate.

Koch, T., and Harrington, A. (1998). 'Reconceptualizing Rigour: The Case for Reflexivity', *Journal of Advanced Nursing*, vol. 28, no. 4: 882-890.

Mead, G.H. (1934) *Mind, Self and Society: From The Standpoint of a Social Behaviorist*, edited by Charles W. Morris, Chicago, University of Chicago Press.

Morley, C. (2004) 'Critical Reflection in Social Work: A Response to Globalisation?', *International Journal of Social Welfare*, vol. 13, no. 4: 297-303.

Payne, M. (2005) *Modern Social Work Theory* 3rd Edition, Hampshire, Palgrave Macmillan.

Plack M.M. and Greenberg L. (2005); 'The Reflective Practitioner: Reaching for Excellence in Practice', *Paediatrics*, vol. 116, no. 6: 1546-1552.

Redmond, B. (2004) 'Reflecting on Practice: Exploring Individual and Organizational Learning Through a Reflective Teaching Model' in N. Gould and M. Baldwin (eds) *Social Work, Critical Reflection and the Learning Organisation*, Aldershot, Ashgate.

Redmond B. and McEvoy, J. (2002) *Learning To Change: A Study of Perceived Changes in Attitudes and Practice of Staff Following their Completion of a Post-Graduate Diploma in Intellectual Disability Studies*, Paper given at IASSID Europe Conference, Dublin June 2002.

Ross, A., King, N. and Firth, R.N. (2005) 'Interprofessional Relationships and Collaborative Working: Encouraging Reflective Practice', *Online Journal of Issues in Nursing*. Vol. 10, No. 1, Manuscript 3. Available: www.nursingworld.org/ojin/topic26/tpc26_3.htm.

Schön, D.A. (1983) *The Reflective Practitioner - How Professionals Think in Action*. New York, Basic Books.

Senge, P. (1992) *The Fifth Discipline*, London, Century Business.

Steier, F. (1991) 'Research as Self-Reflexivity, Self-Reflexivity as Social Process' in F. Steier (ed.), *Research and Reflexivity*, London, Sage.

Taylor, C. and White, S. (2000) *Practising Reflexivity in Health and Welfare: Making Knowledge*, Buckingham, Open University Press.

Williams, B. (2001) 'Developing Critical Reflection for Professional Practice Thought Problem-Based Learning', *Journal of Advanced Nursing*, vol. 34, no. 1: 27-34.

Chapter 1

Introduction

The overall level of satisfaction experienced by service users who access health and social services may often be determined by the authenticity, openness and responsiveness shown to them by individual professionals. However, many service users leave encounters with professionals with feelings of helplessness and a sense that they have neither been listened to nor understood. This may be because, increasingly, many professionals find that limited resources and agency constraints limit their ability to respond fully to client need. However it can also be because the professional perceives the service user only in terms of a specific problem or a theoretical construct, rather than as a unique person with a unique set of issues to be considered (Ming Tsang 1998: 25). Over the past twenty years theorists have suggested that discontinuity between client need and professional response may be rooted in the nature of professional learning and the limitations of professional knowledge. With its emphasis on academic rigour and job-related competencies, professional education tends to produce practitioners who may be theoretically or technically skilled but who have not learned to understand and incorporate the service user's unique perspective into the professional response. The concept of reflective learning for professionals has attempted to address this issue, encouraging professionals to look beyond technical competencies thus enabling them to place the relationship with the service user at the centre of professional practice. Reflective teaching and learning is not confined to the acquisition of new skills, rather it creates an environment where professionals are helped to analyse and re-apprise their practice. The goal of reflective learning is a transformation of perspective (Mezirow 1991) – a significant shift in perspective that allows professionals not only to critically review their practice, but which also helps them to work in a more responsive, creative, and ultimately more effective manner.

This book explores how a reflective teaching and learning environment can bring about positive change in the underlying attitudes to and perceptions of professionals towards those who require their services. It has been claimed that it is easy for the conceptual range of professionals to become progressively more rigid, 'types get set, and experimental generalizations in local circulation are reiterated to the point where they are no longer examined afresh' (Parlett 1991: 222). When such rigidity occurs, it limits the ability of professionals to understand and to respond appropriately and effectively to the needs of their clients. This book explores the extent to which this can occur with professionals and offers new ways of working with professionals which allow them to reconsider their attitudes and practice approaches towards their clients. What follows is an review of the design, implementation and evaluation of a new reflective model of teaching and learning developed with a group of health and social service professionals in a practicum – a learning environment that explores aspects of both theory and practice. In this case, the professionals being researched are a multi-disciplinary group who work with parents of a child or young adult with an intellectual disability (hereinafter referred to as 'parents'). This reflective teaching and learning model has been designed to encourage these professionals to explore their existing perspectives of service users and, by doing so, to be helped to develop more composite, multi-dimensional perspectives of these clients. These perspectives then become the basis upon which professionals can attempt new, more reflective approaches in their work. The model also allows for the support and evaluation of such new approaches.

This book not only monitors the application of the new reflective teaching and learning model, it also observes and analyses the changing role of the reflective teacher within the model. This allows for an exploration of changes in perspective and practice for the professional students during the application of the model and it also investigates what perceptive and practice changes also occur for the researcher/teacher. By appreciating the duality of the researcher/teacher role in this way, the completed model demonstrates its effectiveness in encouraging reflective practice with professional students and also illustrates the reflective characteristics needed by the reflective teacher in its successful application. The design of the reflective teaching model draws on theories of critical learning and reflective practice, especially the work of Donald A. Schön (1983, 1987) and his collaborative work with Chris Argyris (1974, 1996), considered as seminal influences on theories of reflection. Following an analysis of its use in the field of learning disability, the reflective model will be presented as a working model and its transferability to other areas of practice will be proposed.

Background to the Research

My interest in reflection in both practice and education came from my years as a social worker in the services for those with intellectual disability and their families. During that period I had carried out a study of the aspirations, expectations and anxieties of seventy-eight parents who had teenage daughters with intellectual disability (Redmond 1996). This study revealed the parents' overall lack of information about, and involvement in, the service to which their daughter was attached. One of the most significant findings was of a strong perception on the part of parents that their expertise and involvement was not fully valued by the professionals who worked with their children (Redmond 1996: 12-15). The research concluded that, until a genuine working partnership with parents was achieved, parents would continue to experience degrees of isolation, frustration and anger which may only serve to further distance them from the professional staff whom they encountered (Redmond 1996: 78-79).

In subsequent years I moved to a university-based teaching post and continued to meet and work with both individual parents and parents' groups. These contacts consistently revealed mothers and fathers whose dealings with professionals were marked by frustration and conflict. At the same time, I was training staff for work in heath and social services posts and I observed that, although well motivated, many professionals were also experiencing levels of frustration in their ability to work constructively with service users. In a bid to understand the apparent communicative discontinuity between professionals and service users, I became interested in finding ways to encourage professionals to re-examine some of their unconscious or tacit beliefs about service users, which underpinned their practice. I hypothesized that by acknowledging and challenging some of the older underlying professional attitudes towards service users, professionals might find it easier to appreciate the concerns and expectations of those with whom they worked. By doing so, professionals might then alter their practice in order to incorporate such new perspectives. This led me to examine some general theories of reflection and to consider how the adoption of a reflective stance might assist professionals in developing more thoughtful and multi-dimensional perspectives of their clients. Boud et al (1985: 3) described reflection as 'a generic term for those intellectual and affective activities in which individuals engage to explore their experiences in order to lead to new understanding and appreciation'. Mezirow (1991: 104) considered reflection to be the process by which we 'critically assess the content, process or premise(s) of our efforts to interpret and give meaning to an experience'.

In particular, I became drawn to the work of Donald A. Schön (1983, 1987, 1991) and his collaborative work with Chris Argyris (1974, 1996) which was concerned with developing a concept of reflective practice that encouraged professionals to adopt a less 'expert' stance with their clients. Schön (1983: 29) claimed that professionals who were capable of adopting such a reflective approach in their work would, amongst other things, be more responsive to the needs of their clients. He saw the reflective practitioner as being capable of appreciating the uniqueness of the individual client situation and that the working contract forged between reflective professional and service user would be marked by accountability, flexibility and accessibility. For me, Schön's work seemed particularly relevant to the practice and research issues that I was encountering. Schön (1987: 4-5) had indicated that some of the problems with professionals might be inherent in the very nature of professionalism – the application of theory and technique derived from systematic, usually scientific knowledge. He saw that such a notion of professionalism had resulted in some professionals claiming levels of irrefutable expertise that could not be substantiated and he suggested that much professional expertise was cloaked in a degree of mystery and autonomy that distanced the professional from the client. Schön (1983: 288) suggested that the relatively high status of such professional expertise had its roots in the reliance on scientific research, for the most part, in universities and institutes of higher learning.

This notion of the 'expert' professional seemed to correspond to the experiences reported to me by parents in relation to their dealing with professionals (Redmond 1996: 73-74). According to Schön (1983: 290-306) much professional behaviour and its attendant professional language serve to mystify professional knowledge and to confer upon it an autonomy that remove the professional from the need to consult with the client. In what Schön termed the 'technically rational relationship' the expert professional only needed to confer his or her expertise upon the grateful client in order to achieve a successful outcome. Schön (1983: 13-20) considered that the continuing inability or unwillingness of professionals to heed the views of their clients had resulted in a crisis within professions. He saw service users as being increasingly unwilling to tolerate technically rational attitudes from professionals that were patronizing and paternalistic. He argued that the distant, somewhat arrogant stance of technical rationality must be replaced with a far more open, inclusive position where professionals devolve power back to clients/service users, thus engaging them in real partnership (1983: 3-19). He called this reflective practice (1983: 295-307), in which professional and client could work more co-operatively, appreciating the contribution of the individual client to a successful outcome.

I considered that in Schön's image of the reflective professional practitioner lay the attributes necessary for a professional to forge a co-operative partnership with service users in general and with parents of disabled children in particular – these attributes being qualities of empathy, inclusion and respect for the client. However, it was also true that I had encountered many professionals who seemed to have such personal characteristics, but who were still encountering difficulties in their work. I was keen to explore why, despite a genuine concern for service users, some professionals continued to find it hard to fully appreciate the concerns and expectations of those with whom they worked (Manthorpe 1995: 115). Mezirow (1990a: 6-12) had suggested that some professionals operated in a non-reflective state characterized by action that, although thoughtful, lacked a critical examination of underlying beliefs and judgements. Performance in this non-reflective state would be likely to be bounded by habitual practice, a reliance on procedural assumptions and tacit and uncontested perceptions about those whom professionals encounter. If Mezirow's ideas could be applied to the professionals working with parents of disabled children, then by discovering what 'habitual' perceptions of parents were held by professionals I could investigate if these tacit perceptions affected the way in which these professionals interacted with the parents.

Creating a Reflective Research Environment

I was keen to work with professionals in a way that would attempt to bring about a meaningful and lasting change in their perceptions of service users. I also wanted to discover if such work could be usefully undertaken within a university setting where I could create and research a reflective teaching environment that would bring together a number of experienced professionals who were interested in exploring new approaches in their practice. The attraction of the work of Argyris and Schön (1974, 1996) was that it offered me ideas on how to create such a reflective practicum – a classroom-based learning environment where practice issues could be examined and developed. The notion of a practicum offered me an opportunity to create an arena in which to explore the professional/service user relationship in depth, away from the pressures of the workplace, but in an active, participative manner which focused on practice issues. Rather than didactically teaching professionals how best to work with parents I would create what, in Mezirow's (1990b: 368) words, could become a 'separate reality in time and space'. In such a reality the professionals could engage in what Cranton termed 'critical self-reflection' (1994: 159) on their work, exploring aspects of their current practice and being enabled to consider newer, more productive directions.

Establishing the Practicum

In my work as a university lecturer I also had an interest in developing creative teaching techniques that were reflective in nature. In designing this research I wanted to combine the role of reflective teacher with reflective researcher. By doing so I could then monitor how my reflective teaching approach influenced the perspectives held by the professionals in their on-going work with parents. I hypothesized that in such a research environment, the reflective researcher/teacher could challenge such professional students to develop their own reflective capabilities, where they could 'engage critically but openly with the language, conceptual structures and practice traditions being presented to them' (Henkel 1995: 77).

By viewing my role as that of both researcher and teacher, I aimed at designing a model that would not only address and analyse changes in the perspectives of the professional students. Such a model would also incorporate the professionals' changing perspectives into an evolving piece of action research which would impact on my own on-going teaching relationship with them. Thus the research would also address and analyse changes in the perspectives and the practice of the researcher as reflective teacher. This dual role was fundamental to my idea of the practicum where change in both the professionals and in the reflective teacher would be monitored. This would be a practicum where I would challenge the professional students to become more reflective in their practice and where the professional students' responses would equally challenge me to become more reflective in my teaching.

Critical or Transformative Learning

This hypothesis led me to the idea of critical or transformative learning. In order to help professionals recognize the tacit and habitual elements of their practice, it would be necessary to create a reflective environment which would encourage them to critically appraise their current practice and to consider new ways of thinking and feeling about how they operate. Professionals also needed to be encouraged to incorporate and evaluate the validity of such new perspectives in their on-going practice. Mezirow (1991: 6) called this 'perspective transformation' and Brookfield (1987: 27-30) named it 'critical learning'. To help me develop this idea, I drew on the work of theorists in the area of reflection in teaching and critical learning including Jack Mezirow (1981, 1990a, 1990b, 1991), Stephen Brookfield (1987, 1995, 1999) and John Dewey (1902, 1916, 1933, 1974), who was arguably the 'founding father' of reflection. An examination of these theorists' work in the areas of critical learning and perspective transformation offered me possible new directions in teaching approaches which could be used to complement Schön's (1983, 1987) and Argyris's (Argyris and Schön 1974, 1996) notion of the reflective practitioner. The historical evolution of reflection from John Dewey to the present day is dealt with comprehensively in Chapters 2 and 3.

Participative Nature of Research

I wished to design a research approach that would be participative in nature. For me, any research which sought to produce a more equitable and participative relationship between professional and service user should, by its nature, be equitable and participative. I was also keen to monitor my own changing role as reflective teacher within the research. This led me to consider using an action research approach which would allow for the incorporation of such elements in its design. I hypothesized that an action research approach would also complement many elements of both Argyris and Schön's ideas and those of the critical learning theorists. I opted for an action research approach, specifically using Kemmis and McTaggart's *Action Research Planner* (1982), with its cycles of planning, action, observation, reflection and re-planning. I used this research approach over a seven-month period with a group of nineteen professionals attending a one-year, one-day per week postgraduate diploma for professionals working in the area of learning disability. The nineteen students came from different professional backgrounds including nursing, social work, psychology, medicine, occupational therapy and teaching.

Researcher Positioning and the Role of Critical Friends

An important aspect of considering an action research approach is an acknowledgement of the central positioning of the researcher within the research and the possible influence of my presence on any research outcomes. To do so I had to recognize my role in the research dynamic and to monitor and analyse changes in my own perspectives, attitude and demeanour throughout the research process. I decided that, in order to gain an objective and honest appraisal of my own performance, I required assistance from someone familiar with reflective practice so that I could include this element into my research design. To this end I sought the help of two 'critical friends' who were willing to help me monitor my own performance in a reflective manner throughout the research. The idea of a critical friendship relates to a 'learning relationship' forged between peers, sometimes part of a study group, who work together to encourage mutual reflection (Taylor 1997: 103-104). Critical friends can also be skilled reflective practitioners, primarily found in action research settings, who help researchers question the validity of their research explanations and help them maintain a critically self-reflective outlook on their findings (Newman 1999: 3). In this case, both of my two critical friends had extensive expertise of the concept of reflection in general and the theories of Schön in particular. Delong (1996: 7) advised a minimum of two creative critical friends as a support within action research. Critical friends in such a case serve as a sounding board and a source of ideas and encouragement for the researcher. The importance of monitoring what could be termed an 'existential use of self' was noted by Schön (1991: 356), who admonished the reflective researcher to 'remain fully present as a person' within the evolving research dynamic. The record of my reflections on my own role in this research and the support offered to my by the critical friends will be discussed at the end of Chapter 8.

What follows is a record of how this new reflective teaching and learning model was conceived, developed and used within a practicum. It begins with a detailed overview of the process of reflection itself and details the development of reflective ideas from Dewey in the early 20th century up to the present day. The work of Argyris and Schön is explored separately in Chapter 3 and the relationship between reflective theories in general, their reflective theories in particular and the structure of the new reflective teaching model is analysed. The application of the new teaching model with a class of heath and social service professionals is then outlined and the progress of this class over a seven-month period is detailed. The book ends with an evaluation of the reflective teaching model and a critical analysis of the usefulness of such a reflective instrument in the education and training of health and social service professionals

Chapter 2

The Process of Reflection:
An Overview of the Literature

Introduction

This chapter examines the influence and importance of theorists who, each in their own individual way, have played a role in developing the concept of reflection. Authors (Jarvis 1987, 1992, Hemmens 1980, Gowdy 1994, Reece-Jones 1995, Burnard 1995b) who have discussed the concept of reflection in general and the work of Donald A. Schön in particular, have acknowledged the influence of John Dewey, Jürgen Habermas, Paulo Freire and Jack Mezirow on the development of reflection. Dewey (1902, 1916, 1933), Freire (1972, 1973, 1996) and Mezirow (1981, 1990a, 1990b, 1991, 1995) have all played important roles in developing a view of learning as a transformatory process through which individuals are encouraged to critically assess their interpretations of experience (Cranton 1994: 48). Stephen Brookfield (1987, 1990, 1993, 1995; Brookfield and Preskill 1999) has looked at the significance of reflection for the adult learner and has further developed the idea of the transformatory nature of learning. Brookfield (1995) has also examined the specific issues for those who aspire to teach in a way which encourages critically reflective learning in their students.

Freire (1972, 1996) examined the power of reflection in education, seeing it as an emancipatory force for the weak and powerless. Habermas (1971, 1984) also developed the notion that through reflective thought a full understanding of dominant political and social forces offers freedom for the individual. Habermas warned that professionals have immense potential, if not actual power, and an awareness of the use and abuse of such power is vital for all those who deliver services, not least for the professionals themselves (Henkel 1995: 74). In terms of the development of this reflective teaching and learning model for professionals in health and social services, such an insight is vital in enabling those professionals to appreciate the wider dimensions to their relationships with clients.

Dewey, Habermas, Freire, Mezirow and Brookfield all developed concepts of reflection which have particular significance in illuminating not only the work of Donald A. Schön but also for understanding the design of the reflective teaching and learning model explored in this book. I have included elements of the five theorists' work in the construction of the specific phases in my reflective teaching and learning model. This chapter will discuss, in some detail, the work of these seminal theorists and will then look more concisely at the work of other writers such as George Kelly (1955), Michael Polanyi (1967), and David Boud (Boud et al 1985, Boud and Walker 1998, Boud 1999). These authors have either contributed to the idea of reflection or have advanced aspects of reflection into new forms and models. The chapter ends with an account of both the chronology and the interrelation between major theorists in the field.

John Dewey

In examining the development of the concept of reflection, it would be impossible not to view John Dewey as a major influence: 'perhaps the most significant of all writers who have expressed their ideas on this subject [reflective learning] is John Dewey' (Jarvis 1987: 87). John Dewey is often referred to as the father of modern American education, but his ideas and philosophies underpin major educational systems on a world wide basis (Tsuin-Chen 1970: 339-364).

Born in 1859, Dewey was a teacher, philosopher, psychologist and educationalist who continued teaching and writing until shortly before his death in 1952 at the age of ninety-two. As well as his many other achievements in a long and distinguished career, Mezirow (1991: 100) claims that Dewey made the seminal analysis of reflection. Dewey (1933: 9) saw the act of reflection as central to human learning and personal development and he defined reflection as 'active, persistent and careful consideration of any belief or supposed form of knowledge in the light of the grounds that support it and the further conclusion to which it tends'. He viewed human experience as central to reflection, but experience 'as an active and future-oriented rather than a passive and past-oriented concept' (Henkel 1995: 71).

For Dewey (1933: 100-101), intelligence was not necessarily an innate quality, but one that could be developed and honed as individuals responded to experience through the process of reflective thought. He named such a response 'reflection' and thought it capable of transforming a situation 'in which there is experienced obscurity, doubt, conflict, disturbance of some sort, into a situation that is clear, settled, harmonious'. Dewey's work became critical in building theories of learning in general and of adult education in particular (Cranton 1994: 6). Two pieces of Dewey's work of special significance in understanding his view of reflection are his *Democracy and Education* (1916) and *How We Think* (1933). The former work demonstrates Dewey's partialisation of experience, which he felt was the organizing focus for learning. Dewey argued that observations and actions are synthesized with conceptual ideas leading to higher-order practice (Gould 1996a: 2) – a view very much echoed by Schön's partialisation of reflective practice (1983: 49-69). The partialisation of the reflective process is an important aspect of the design of this reflective teaching and learning model where I have monitored the individual reflective 'journeys' taken by each participant in the research.

Trial, Error and Reflection

The essence of Dewey's 'reflective activity' in learning can be found in *How We Think* (1933): the presence of two kinds of experiential processes – lower-order trial and error and the higher level of reflection, leading to the creation of a learning loop (Boud et al 1985: 11). This notion of the learning loop is central to Argyris and Schön's concept of Model I and Model II practice (to be discussed in chapter 3), which is incorporated in the design of the reflective teaching and learning model in this book. Argyris and Schön (1992: xiii) argued that behind any piece of interpersonal action lies that actor's theories-in-use (his ways of behaving and of rationalizing his behaviour) which are usually tacit, acquired in early life and difficult to change. Argyris and Schön (1974: 63-134) describe an action as Model I when the actor does not move beyond his original theory-in-use, even which his actions do not achieve what he wants to achieve. They define an action as Model II when the actor reflects on the suitability of his theory-in-use and subsequently alters his behaviour in order to achieve his goal. Argyris and Schön refer to this reflection and change in behaviour as 'double-loop learning'.

Routine and Capricious Thought and Schön's Knowing-In-Action

For Dewey (1916: 140), the absence of reflection reduces an activity to that of a blind or capricious impulse, with nothing in the experience to connect it to any prior activity of the individual. 'There is no before or after to such experience; no retrospect nor outlook and consequently no meaning.' Dewey's view of routine or capricious thought reappears in what Schön (1987: 26) called 'knowing-in-action': 'When we have learned to do something we can execute smooth sequences of activity, recognition, decision and adjustment without having, as we say, to "think about it". Our spontaneous knowing-in-action usually gets us through the day. On occasion, however, it doesn't.' Dewey (1902: 481) warned of the seductive comfort and danger of routine action without reflection when he stated: 'Familiarity breeds contempt, but it also breeds something like affection. We get used to the chains we wear and miss them when removed ... unpleasant, because meaningless, activities may get agreeable if long enough persisted in.'

Dewey saw reflection as the discernment of the relationship between what we try to do and what happens in consequence. Dewey (1916: 150-151) indicated that such a reflective stance would be more likely to occur when routine or habitual practice did not work as planned. This would lead to confusion or doubt that, in turn, would encourage the practitioner to re-examine and question previous actions. This is the action of reflection that should then lead individuals to attempt new forms of behaviour. One of the goals of this reflective teaching and learning model has been to encourage professionals to recognize the routine, implicit skills in their practice, which tend to be delivered without conscious deliberation or a deeper questioning of the wider situation within which the practitioner is operating.

Characteristics of Reflective Thought

Dewey viewed reflective thinking as being composed of distinctive features or characteristics which he developed from his early writing on the *Child and the Curriculum* (1902), reappearing in both *Democracy and Education* (1916) and *The Way We Think* (1933). These characteristics are important because later writers (Mezirow 1981, Brookfield 1987) have used similar or related characteristics in their own work. A compilation of these features drawn from a number of Dewey's works is shown below:

- The suggestion that a piece of normal or habitual behaviour is not working to plan – a realization that something is wrong. This awareness is accompanied by an impulsive, anticipatory assessment of what this situation seems to predict – what will happen if the original course of action continues.
- Critical consideration of relevant data to analyse all aspects of the problematic situation. This is when the intellectualization of the problem commences.
- Formation of different hypotheses to deal with the situation.
- Sorting these hypotheses, and choosing the one which seems most effective.
- Testing the hypothesis.
- Reflecting on whether another hypothesis or action could have resolved the situation more effectively.

Adapted from Dewey (1916: 150-151; 1933: 100-103) and Axtelle and Burnett (1970: 265).

Dewey (1933: 105) made clear that these characteristics do not necessarily follow each other in strict order. 'In practice, two of them may telescope, some may be passed over hurriedly and the burden of reaching a conclusion may fall mainly on a single phase ... no set rules can be laid down on such matters. The way they are managed depends upon the intellectual tact and sensitivity of the individual.' It is important to note that in Dewey's work on the partialisation of reflective thinking can be found all the characteristics of the stages in Mezirow's phases of transformation (1991: 168), Brookfield's phases of critical thinking (1987: 25) and Schön's reflective practice (1983: 49-69) – all of which will be discussed later.

The Reflective Practicum

It is in the formation of the research practicum, a 'setting designed for the task of learning a practice' (Schön 1987: 37), that Dewey can be seen as such an important influence on Schön's reflective practicum (1987: 305), Mezirow's transformative learning environment (1991: 219) and Brookfield's critically reflective classroom (1995: 94). Developing on from Dewey's partialisation of the process of reflection, it is within the practicum that Dewey's phases of the learning process can be seen, appreciated and allowed to become a medium for learning and change. Dewey

(1974: 7) envisaged that the practicum would provide an environment for 'the practical work of modification, of changing, of reconstruction continued without end'.

Lastly, Dewey demonstrated (1974: 181-182) within the reflective practicum how the research practitioner can study the reflective processes at work and how these processes can be used effectively to develop true professional artistry. Dewey saw the importance of the reflective teacher/coach who would also function as a reflective researcher within the practicum. He noted that the role of the reflective teacher/coach would always have an influence on the students in the practicum and that this influence needed to be noted and incorporated in the reflective process. 'Everything the teacher does, as well as the manner in which he does it, incites the [student] to respond in some way or other ... the teacher is rarely (and even then never entirely) a transparent medium of access by another mind to a subject' (Dewey 1933: 47-48).

Dewey (1974: 181) outlined the factors necessary for studying the sophisticated and subtle nuances of reflective practice. These were the causal conditions of learning – the candour and sincerity necessary to keep track of failures and the acute observation needed to judge progress 'more than is needed to note the results of mechanically applied tests'. Dewey was demonstrating that the act of thinking is, in itself, a process of inquiry and investigation and that research should be recognized not as a rarefied activity, but as a common occurrence of the thinker. 'We sometimes talk as if "original research" were a peculiar prerogative of scientists or at least of advanced students. But all thinking is research, and all research is native, original, with him who carries it on, even if everybody else in the world already is sure of what he is looking for' (Dewey 1916: 148).

Cranton (1994: 48) has suggested that the ideas of reflective learning and reflective education, as articulated in recent literature, have not deviated conceptually from Dewey's original vision. Dewey (1933: 89-90) proposed that every learning episode should be considered as one which is a 'reconstruction or reorganization of experience which adds to the meaning of experience, and which increases ability to direct the course of subsequent experience'. His idea was that reflection allowed individuals to see through the habitual way the experience of everyday life is interpreted. By doing so it is possible to reassess the implicit claim of validity made by a previously unquestioned meaning scheme or perspective (Mezirow 1991: 102). Dewey's view of reflection is central to the reflective teaching and learning model developed in this book. So also are his ideas on the role of the reflective teacher who should, in Dewey's view (1916: 186-188), be less concerned with the presentation of facts than in the creation of a learning environment which stimulates the student to reach new levels of discovery. In this way, it can be seen that I have tried to incorporate what Bernstein described as the 'spirit of Dewey' (1985: 58) in the design of this model for reflective teaching and learning.

Jürgen Habermas

Dewey identified that, when an action takes place without reflection, such an action is reduced to a habitual or capricious impulse. In a similar vein, Jürgen Habermas (1971: 310) identified the importance of recognizing unjust dominant ideologies that are likely to be uncritically accepted and are embedded in everyday situations and practices. Such unjust ideologies become part of language, social habits and cultural norms and they legitimize certain social structures and educational practices so that they are accepted as normal (Brookfield 1995: 87).

Habermas's work *Knowledge and Human Interest* (first published 1968, translated 1971) is important because, like Dewey, Habermas attempted to partialise the learning process. In *Knowledge and Human Interest* Habermas (1971: 308-310) saw three generic areas where human interest could generate knowledge, three different ways of perceiving and understanding the world – technical, practical and emancipatory. These categories, which Habermas called 'cognitive' or 'knowledge guiding' interests, each possess different methodologies of systematic objective enquiry. Jack Mezirow (1981: 4), a key figure in the development of adult education, saw Habermas's three categories as being of vital importance for his own work. 'Each learning domain suggests to me a different mode of personal learning and different learning needs, I believe Habermas's work is seminal for understanding both learning and education'. Part of Mezirow's attraction to Habermas's work in general and his three categories of learning in particular, was its suitability in the sphere of adult education (Mezirow 1991: 64-68). In the same way Habermas's work also has relevance for this researcher in her work with adult professionals. Therefore, Habermas's three categories form part of the rationale for the design of the different phases in this researcher's reflective teaching and learning model. A close examination of Habermas's three areas of cognitive interest shows how each offers a separate concept of 'knowing' and 'learning'.

1. Technical Learning Domain Knowing within this category is based on empirical wisdom and is controlled by technical rules, this area is governed by instrumental action. Habermas saw hypotheses in this category tending to involve observable events where results can be proved as being correct or incorrect. These 'empirical-analytic' sciences are governed by technical control of objectified processes: 'the facts relevant to the empirical sciences are first constituted through an a priori organization of experience in the behavioural system of instrumental action (Habermas 1984: 327). This domain belongs to the empirical-analytic sciences including areas of medicine, physics, actuarial disciplines and computer technologies.

2. Practical Learning Domain Knowing within this area is characterized by 'communicative action'. Unlike the more technical instrumental action depending upon empirical-analytic truth, collective action depends on systematic enquiry that seeks to understand meaning and looks to hermeneutics, the science of interpretation and explanation. 'Access to the facts is provided by an understanding of meaning, not observation. The verification of lawlike hypotheses in empirical-analytic sciences has its counterpart here in the interpretation of texts. Thus the rules of hermeneutics determine the possible meaning of the validity of statements in the cultural sciences' (Habermas 1984: 309). This is, therefore, the domain of the hermeneutic sciences of history, law, psychology, literature and sociology.

3. Emancipatory Learning Domain   It is primarily in this third category that we see Habermas develop his interest in reflection, as he moves from the empirical sciences, through hermeneutic interpretation to the domain of self-knowledge. What makes this third area so different is Habermas's view that, through knowledge gained via self-reflection, it is possible for individuals to free themselves from the forces which limit their ability to succeed and become fully powerful. In this way, Habermas saw critical reflection to be a means of emancipation (Habermas 1984: 310).

In simple terms, Habermas saw that knowledge in the empirical domain led to control, knowledge in the hermeneutic domain led to understanding, but knowledge in the emancipatory domain led to real freedom. Freedom becomes possible because emancipatory knowledge embraces critical reflection which allows for an appreciation of the forces which control, subtly or overtly, the ability to realize full human potential (Cranton 1994: 46). These controls may be social, racial, gender-based, economic, religious or political – it is only when individuals grasp how such ideologies frame and define their life expectations that real change becomes possible. Habermas (1971: 310-311) considered that emancipatory learning also leads to a questioning of how such powerful ideologies may appear benign, protective and in society's best interests, yet may really serve as powerful agents of social control. Emancipatory knowledge offers insight into lawlike conditions and initiates a process of reflection in the consciousness of those whom the laws seek to control (Mezirow 1981: 4-5). By this process a reflective, or critical consciousness is developed which can then judge such laws as being appropriate or inappropriate.

Bernstein saw the importance of Habermas as being on a par with that of Dewey: 'no less than John Dewey, Habermas is a philosopher of democracy' (1991: 207). Like Schön, Habermas himself acknowledged his own debt to the work of Dewey, declaring that he had long identified himself with Dewey's radical democratic mentality (1985: 198). Bernstein (1991: 48) agreed with Habermas's acknowledgement of Dewey's influence: 'both share an understanding of rationality as intrinsically dialogical and communicative and both pursue the ethical and political consequences of this form of rationality.' To clarify this statement, Mezirow (1991: 26) interpreted Habermas's use of the term rationality to mean a process of achieving mutual understanding by actively assessing the validity and cogency of an argument.

It is interesting that Habermas, like Dewey, also emerges as an important influence on many of the later theorists in the areas of reflective learning and reflective practice. Habermas's philosophy of emancipatory knowledge, although not formally acknowledged by Schön, clearly exists in his vision of the reflective practitioner. Schön's frame analysis (1983: 309-314), discussed later in greater detail, argues that when a practitioner forms an understanding of his frame – his construction of reality – then a change in that frame can occur. In this way previously held certainties can be open to reflection and change. Just as Habermas's emancipatory 'knower' can reflect on his world, see its limiting frames and choose transformation, so Schön's reflective practitioner can choose to reflect upon and change the frames which constrain his ability to respond creatively to his client.

Brookfield (1993: 228-230) saw Habermas's work as being especially significant in the formation of a theory of critical learning in adult education. Although they differ in some detail, Mezirow's learning domain – instrumental learning, communicative learning and emancipatory learning (1991: 72-89) – show a great similarity to Habermas's technical learning, practical learning and emancipatory learning domains. However, Mezirow (1991: xiv) states that he has not 'attempted to interpret systematically what Habermas or any other single theorist has to say about adult learning'. An examination of Habermas's writing helps to illuminate the work of Mezirow in particular and to add depth to an understanding of Schön's work on reflection. Most particularly, Habermas's three domains of learning (1971: 308-317) offer a different and challenging perspective which has been incorporated into my design of a reflective teaching and learning model.

Jack Mezirow

As discussed above, Mezirow (1991: 65) acknowledges the importance of Habermas's work in understanding adult learning and the functions and goals of adult education. Mezirow has also been influenced by Schön, acknowledging Schön's work on professional learning in his own development of perspective transformation (Mezirow 1991: 185). However, of all the reflective theorists, Mezirow has been particularly receptive to the writing of Freire and he acknowledges that his own personal 'conscientization', which resulted from reading Freire, altered the course of his life (1995: 8). Mezirow's own writings have also led to exciting new theoretical developments in the field of adult education (Cranton 1994: 1).

Perspective Transformation and Critical Reflection

Just as both Habermas (1971: 308-309) and Schön (1983: 309-310) see that emancipation begins with true awareness of the individual's frames of reference, Mezirow saw the importance of transforming the individual's 'meaning perceptions

– the structure of assumptions that constitutes a frame of reference for interpreting the meaning of an experience' (Mezirow et al 1990: xvi). Mezirow also saw 'perspective transformation' as an emancipatory process 'of becoming critically aware of how and why the structure of psycho-cultural assumptions has come to constrain the way we see ourselves and our relationships, reconstituting this structure to permit a more inclusive and discriminating integration of experience and acting upon these new understandings' (Mezirow 1981: 6). Mezirow equated his perspective transformation with Freire's 'conscientization' and Habermas's 'emancipatory action' and saw it as a central function of adult learning and education (Mezirow 1981: 6; 1991: 37-63).

Mezirow believed that the process of transforming an individual's frames of reference begins with critical reflection. While all reflection involves elements of appraisal and contemplation, critical reflection demands that firmly held presumptions and suppositions are also scrutinized 'critical reflection addresses the question of the justification for the very premises on which problems are posed or defined in the first place' (Mezirow 1990a: 12).

Mezirow's Seven Levels of Critical Reflectivity

Given the importance placed by Mezirow on critical reflection and its crucial role in adult learning and in perspective transformation, he felt that critical reflection required phenomenological study. To this end he devised a construct of critical reflectivity consisting of seven levels (Mezirow 1981: 11-13).

The steps of Mezirow's model (1981: 12-13) start with the most basic level of awareness:

1. Reflectivity   Simple awareness of behaviour, perception or meaning through seeing, thinking and action (and habits of same).

2. Affective Reflectivity Becoming aware of how one feels about one's perceptions, thoughts and actions (and habits of same).

3. Discriminant Reflectivity   Assessing the efficacy of one's perceptions, thoughts and actions; identifying causes and recognizing reality contexts in which one functions and the relationships which exist within such contexts.

4. Judgemental Reflectivity   Making and becoming aware of one's value judgements, perceptions, thoughts and actions in terms of their place in a value continuum – strong or weak, useful or useless, positive or negative. Such value judgements bear similarities to the emergent/submergent poles of Kelly's personal constructs as articulated in repertory grids (Kelly 1955, 1965 , 1969, Francella and Bannister 1977), discussed later in this chapter.

Whereas points 1 to 4 have come under the category of 'consciousness', Mezirow now moves critical reflection into what is called meta-learning or meta-cognition

(Mezirow 1990a: 8), the sphere of 'critical consciousness' where individuals become aware of their own awareness.

5. Conceptual Reality Deciding if the value judgements or concepts (see point 4) one uses are appropriate or adequate to understand or judge a particular case. For example one may decide a particular service provision is either good or bad, but do these concepts help assess if the usefulness or appropriateness of such a service is appropriate or useful for one's particular needs at this point?

6. Psychic Reality Recognizing in oneself the habit of making precipitate judgements on the basis of limited information, 'judging the book by the cover' but *knowing* that one tends to do so, especially in particular circumstances of which one is aware.

7. Theoretical Reflectivity Realizing that one's tendency towards such precipitative judgements (see point 6) exists because cultural, psychological or social pressures have encouraged one to reach such instinctive and unproductive conclusions. Theoretical reflection encourages such awareness and also allows for changes in perspective to occur leading to 'more functional criteria for seeing, thinking and acting' (Mezirow 1981: 13). This then allows for full perspective transformation and full emancipation. Again, we have reached Habermas's level of reflective (critical) consciousness.

Perspective Transformation and Adult Learning

Mezirow's later work (1990, 1991, 1995) further developed his ideas on perspective transformation and adult education. He began to see the ability to operate within the realm of critical consciousness as purely an adult function and maintained that only adults were capable of perspective transformation. 'Perspective transformation appears to best account for the process of transition between stages of adult psychological development in major life span theories' (Mezirow 1981: 13). This concurs with Basseches' theory (1984: 22) that certain modes of thinking, which include perspective transformation, are only achieved in the late adolescent and adult years. Labouvie-Vief and Blanchard-Fields (1984: 169) also identified differences in cognition and perspective transformation ability between younger and older adults. They noted that older adults are less likely to accept tasks at face value, are less likely to perform in compliance with authority and tend to evaluate task structures in relation to their social and personal goals. This qualitative difference between younger and older adults' capacity for perspective transformation and its subsequent effect on personal reflection was significant in Mezirow's work in adult education. It also has relevance especially in relation to facilitating professionals of varying ages to address levels of reflection within their own work.

Boud, Keogh and Walker (1985: 23) make the connection between the perspective transformation of Mezirow and the term 'conscientization', used by Freire to describe the process by which one's false consciousness becomes transcended through education. As this chapter moves on to look at the importance of Freire in developing the concept of reflection it becomes clear that reflection can be seen as a means of enhancing self-awareness and enablement. Not only that – for some theorists it has become an integral part of a theory of human liberation.

Paulo Freire

The inclusion of Paulo Freire in this discussion is important because of the value of his contribution to the development of the concept of reflection which is connected to previous and subsequent theorists discussed in this chapter.

Born in 1921 in northeast Brazil, Freire witnessed a community of extreme poverty and illiteracy living in what he saw as a 'culture of silence'. Trained as a philosopher and educationalist, he co-ordinated the Brazilian National Literacy Programme in the early 1960s, bringing about substantial improvements in rates of adult literacy – highly significant in a country where only the literate could vote. Following a military coup in 1964, Freire was imprisoned on charges of fostering an educational policy opposed to the national interest. He then went into exile where he wrote, amongst other works, his seminal work, *Pedagogy of the Oppressed* (Freire 1972).

This biographical sketch of Freire illustrates the rationale for his commitment to education and empowerment and his concerns about the submissive tendencies of people living within oppressive power structures. Freire saw that the oppressive regimes encouraged habits of submission and docility which caused individuals to cease questioning their life circumstances and to accept the unacceptable (Weiler 1994: 13). Like Habermas's critical reflection, Mezirow's critical consciousness and Dewey's reflective thinking, Freire (1972: 81) saw the development of critical thought and reflection as essential to emancipation and liberation: 'reflection upon situationality is reflection about the very condition of existence.'

For Freire, education represented a powerful liberating force, but he warned against a type of education which exists without reflection, which he termed the 'banking concept of education'. In this system 'knowledge is a gift bestowed by those who consider themselves knowledgeable upon those who they consider know nothing' (1972: 46). The banking concept of education portrays the teacher as powerful, knowledgeable and dynamic; conversely the student appears passive, ignorant and accepting. Freire argues that the banking concept of education has a directly negative effect on the ability of the individual to develop critical consciousness. The more the student engages in this type of education, the less he will question its validity and the more he will accept it as the only reality of knowledge (Heaney and Horton 1990: 84-85).

Freire felt that critical reflection would allow the individual to appraise, recreate and improve his own reality. However, many experiencing oppression had become so entrenched in social norms that they had lost the self-confidence and the ability to question or challenge their direction or destiny (Rivage-Seul and Rivage-Seul 1994: 46-47). This lack of confidence is nurtured, in no small part, by an autocratic banking style of education. To escape from such imposed docility, Freire felt that education had to be 'problem-posing'. This style of education must attempt to break the vertical, authoritarian, didactic characteristics of banking education and become a circular dialogue between student and teacher. 'The teacher is no longer merely the-one-who-teaches, but one who is himself taught in dialogue with the students, who in their turn while being taught also teach' (Freire 1972: 53). The importance of the reflective teacher, as well as the reflective student, is central to Freire's philosophy of emancipation. He argued that the teacher should not perceive knowledge as solely his domain, but should enter a relationship with students where they become part of a co-investigative dialogue, where 'the problem-posing educator constantly re-forms his reflections in the reflection of the student' (Freire 1972: 54).

Freire saw this problem-posing model as leading to 'conscientization', the ability to critically appreciate one's own place in the larger social schema. Where banking education maintained the 'submersion' of consciousness, problem-posing education created the 'emergence' of consciousness and critical intervention in reality (Mezirow 1991: 135). However, Freire saw that reflection would also be a precursor of action and he called the relationship between reflection and action 'praxis'. He warned that reflection on its own, with no opportunity for action or change, became 'verbalism': 'an alienated and alienating "blah"' (Freire 1972: 60) and action without reflection was action for action's sake: 'activism'. Freire wanted both reflection and action to come together in dialogue to 'name the world': 'Men are not built in silence, but in word, in work, in reflection-action' (Freire 1972: 61).

On examination, Freire's philosophy seems seductively simple, but Mezirow (1981: 7-9) warns that the process of conscientization may be beset by stumbling blocks which Freire does not acknowledge. The most significant of these is Freire's failure to acknowledge the difficulties inherent in perspective transformation. 'Although one does not return to an old perspective once a transformation occurs, this passage involves a difficult negotiation and compromise – stalling, backsliding, self-deception are exceedingly common' (Mezirow 1981: 8). Also Freire does not develop a theory on the process of reflection, instead he hypothesizes that, given the correct educational environment, critical reflection and conscientization will occur. Unlike other theorists, Freire does no attempt to partialise or investigate the process of reflection itself. In spite of this, Freire offers a deeply sustained philosophy which is revolutionary both socially and individually and his writing, with its compulsion and integrity, may well compel readers to achieve new levels of personal reflection.

Before his death in 1997 Freire re-visited his influential *Pedagogy of the Oppressed* and, in *Pedagogy of Hope* (1996), he clarified some of the central elements espoused in his earlier work. Specifically in *Pedagogy of Hope* Freire looked at the importance of a democratic relationship between student and teacher. In such a relationship the teacher needs to strive to understand the process of critical thought being undertaken by students and to develop his/her own critical faculties which must also be shared with students (1996: 119). Finally Freire reiterated his belief that teaching and research are inextricably linked in the university classroom, an important aspect of my own perception of myself as teacher and researcher.

> The circle of knowledge has but two moments, in permanent relationship with each other: the moment of the cognition of existing already-produced knowledge and the moment of our own production of new knowledge. There is no genuine instruction in whose process no research is performed by way of question, investigation, curiosity, creativity; just as there is no research in the course of which researchers do not learn (Freire 1996: 192-193).

Stephen Brookfield

The final author whose work is dealt with in some detail in this chapter is Stephen Brookfield. Brookfield writes frankly, from a personal perspective, about the considerable challenges which face any teacher who aims at becoming more reflective.

Brookfield and Mezirow have developed very similar ideas on critical reflection. Both authors have been primarily engaged in developing critical reflection in the area of adult education (Brookfield 1988, 1995, 1999; Mezirow 1990a, 1990b, 1991). Mezirow has also published with Brookfield and has included an article by him on critical incidences (Brookfield 1990: 177-193) in Mezirow's edited work on fostering critical reflection in adulthood (Mezirow et al 1990). Mezirow admired Brookfield's strategies for facilitating critical thinking in a classroom, especially his work on critical questioning (Mezirow 1990b: 374): Brookfield notes that both he and Mezirow agree on the importance of learners seeing the process of critical reflection modelled for them by a credible teacher (Brookfield 1995: 205).

Components of Critical Thought

Brookfield identified four components which must be present if thinking is to be termed 'critical' (1987: 7-9):

1. Identifying and challenging assumptions Brookfield saw that the assumptions, which sustain ideas, beliefs and action, need to be identified so that critical thinkers can examine their accuracy and validity.

2. *Challenging the importance of context* Critical thinkers need to become aware that actions are never context-free and critical thinkers need to become contextually aware.

3. *Exploring alternative actions* Central to critical thinking is the ability to imagine and to explore alternative ways of thinking and acting.

4. *Becoming reflectively sceptical* Being reflectively sceptical means that the critical thinker learns to question fixed beliefs, habitual behaviours and entrenched social structures. As Brookfield says: 'critical thinkers will become immediately suspicious of those who say they have the answers to all life's problems' (1987: 9).

Brookfield has also suggested levels of critical learning (1987: 25-29) which bear considerable similarity to those outlined by Mezirow's stages of reflection (1981: 11-16). I have drawn from these five in the design of this reflective teaching and learning model. They include:

- a trigger event which prompts inner discomfort or perplexity
- a period of self-scrutiny or appraisal following the trigger event
- an exploration of ways to explain discrepancies produced by the discrepancy
- the development of alternative perspectives on possible new ways of behaving
- the integration of the these new approaches into one's life.

Cranton (1994: 62) considers that Brookfield's work reveals him to be the closest of the current theorists to Mezirow, noting that Brookfield's conceptualization of critical thinking is analogous to Mezirow's description of transformative learning. However, in his later works, Brookfield has developed these ideas of critical thinking further, exploring ways in which students can reach these levels of critical thinking with the help of what he terms the 'critically reflective teacher' (1995). Brookfield's strengths lie in his ability to discuss critical reflection at a theoretical level while also developing skills useful for the practical application of a critically reflective teaching environment. Brookfield has also explored the use of discussion as a way of teaching at university level (Brookfield and Preskill 1999), again with both theoretical and practical perspectives on the topic.

Brookfield's work on developing critically reflective teaching practices, especially his personal accounts of his own attempts to become more aware of the assumptions behind his teaching are insightful. Brookfield (1995: xv) describes his writing as being accessible and personal, with a wish to connect to his readers viscerally as well as intellectually. His work, which includes helpful examples from his own practice, has a refreshing immediacy and honesty. He believes that a process as complex as critical reflection needs to be grounded as much as possible in the description of concrete events and actions (1995: xvi). In my own attempts to maintain a perceptive and honest view of my performance as a teacher, I have found solace in Brookfield's candour about his own successes and failures at developing reflection in his teaching practice.

Dewey, Mezirow, Habermas, Freire and Brookfield have all developed the concept of reflection in diverse and stimulating ways. There are other theorists who have added different perspectives on the concept of reflection and who have also begun to develop new models based on reflective philosophies. The rest of the chapter will examine such work, making connections to the work of the theorists already discussed. Exploring reflective theory in this direction leads eventually to the work of Donald A. Schön who for the first time moved the ideas of critical learning beyond the realms of education and developed a model of reflection that was applicable to any form of profession practice. Schön's work will be discussed in the next chapter. It should also be noted that the work of Chris Argyris, although relevant to this section, will be discussed in the next chapter due to his closeness to and frequent co-authorship with Schön.

Common themes emerge in the writings of Dewey, Habermas, Mezirow, Freire and Schön which deal with the individual's perception of his or her culture. They also look at the meaning he/she ascribes to that existence and how such perceptions and meanings can be incorporated into an act of critical reflection if real change and learning is to occur. Mezirow's work on perspective transformation (1991: 150-185), Freire's conscientization (1972: 27); Brookfield's contextual awareness (1987: 8) and Schön's frame reflection (1983: 309-315) all deal with acknowledging the meaning individuals ascribe to their existence. Habermas and Dewey also deal with the individual construction of meanings and both he and Mezirow examine the role of language as a primary conveyor of meaning where language displays vital symbolic constructs and methods of understanding that are culturally transmitted, developed and sanctioned (Mezirow 1991: 57).

The five major theorists discussed above have offered different ways of viewing the nature of reflection. The foregoing review of their work also reveals common themes that emerge in their work on the phases or stages of reflection. Figure 2.1 compares the stages of reflection as conceived by Dewey, Mezirow, Habermas and Brookfield. Freire has not been included in this grid because, as has been noted in this chapter, he tended to view reflection as a single activity, without any constituent phases. This grid will be subsequently used, in Chapter 7, as the basis of the phases used in my own reflective teaching and learning model.

Figure 2.1 Comparison of Stages of Reflective Learning I

Dewey	Habitual Action	New data to inform situation	Intellectualisation of problem Formulation of new hypothesis	Testing of new hypothesis	Reflection & evaluation of hypotheses
Mezirow	Unresolved dilemma based on habitual assumption	Trigger event	Perspective transformation	Emancipatory learning	Reflection on transformation
Habermas	Technical practice Objectified Processes	Exposure to new ideologies	Reassessment of previous meanings	Emancipatory learning domain	Emancipatory learning with self-reflection
Brookfield	Habitual working practices	Trigger event	Discomfort, exploration of old working practices	Development of alternative perspectives	Integration of new approaches

Other Perspectives on Reflection

George Kelly

Gould (1996a: 7) has observed that debates within social theory have demonstrated an interest 'in how imagery and metaphor operate as schemas through which the individual organizes his or her knowledge of the world and acts within it'. Gould has used George Kelly's repertory grid as a way of facilitating reflection in social work students, to help them to become more aware of the assumptions that they brought to their practice and their likelihood to stereotype people and their behaviour (Gould 1996b: 73).

George Kelly (1955: 560-561) suggested that individual perspectives may be composed of dichotomous constructs resulting from past experiences. It has already been noted that Mezirow's 'judgmental reflectivity' bears a resemblance to Kelly's constructs where the unique perspectives of the individual exist on a value continuum ranging between alternative poles – good/bad, helpful/unhelpful, frightening/friendly. Kelly saw such constructs, deriving from past experiences, as 'a personal theory being put to the test' (Bannister and Fransella 1971: 27). He saw that individuals need to develop an approach in order to understand how they react to, think and feel about the world and, to this end, he developed the repertory grid (Kelly 1955). Gould (1996b: 71) argues that there are interesting parallels between Schön's epistemology of reflective practice and Kelly personal construct theory. He sees both Schön and Kelly as contributing to theories of knowledge with the practitioner/professional in the role of action/researcher 'testing out and modifying hypotheses in the process of intervention'.

Candy (1990: 284) suggests that Kelly's repertory grid offers an adaptable tool that has applications in many areas, with individuals or groups, in therapeutic situations or in the study of the learning process. The repertory grid is not the only tool relevant to reflective practice and Harri-Augustine and Thomas (1991: 267-293) outline a broader taxonomy of reflective tools, all based within the personal construct model, which help understand and interpret personal meaning and reflection on experience. However, in terms of the usefulness of Kelly's repertory grid, Candy (1990: 290) argues that when the grid is used 'in a sensitive, thoughtful and reflective way by people interested in enhancing their self-understanding, it can be a powerful aid to transformative learning'.

Michael Polanyi and Tacit Knowing

Like Kelly's work on personal construct theory, Michael Polanyi (1967) developed a theory of tacit knowledge that is aimed at making explicit the implicit constructs which controlled the individual's view of the world. In terms of the reflective professional, Polanyi developed a concept that described how individuals 'know' certain things but cannot explicitly explain how or why they hold such knowledge (Polanyi 1967). For example, cooks will remark that they know when a dish is ready 'by the look of it' but find it impossible to specify exactly what this characteristic of readiness is. Likewise a potter may not be able to explain how she knows why a piece of clay 'feels right' when making a pot, but such tacit sensibilities, vital for her craft, still remain implicit. Polanyi calls this 'tacit knowing' or the holding of an informal theory. Much informal theory is based on unexplained knowledge and Polanyi sees the need to reflect on implicit, tacit knowledge thus starting a process which works towards making explicit what we already know.

The importance of Polanyi's theory of tacit knowing is also the perception of tacit knowledge as an important and separate part of learning, something hidden which can be discovered. Polanyi's theory has relevance for situations where practitioners may be guided by implicit practice wisdom, but have no means of testing either the reliability of such knowledge or of passing it on to anybody else in a planned way. In relation to Polanyi's work, Argyris and Schön (1974: 11) comment that 'when we formulate our theories-in-use [tacit/implicit knowledge] we are making explicit what we know tacitly; we can test our explicit knowledge against our tacit knowledge just as the scientist can test his explicit hypothesis against his intimations'. What needs to be added is that such recognition and testing of tacit knowledge can only take place in reflection.

David Boud

David Boud and his colleagues took Kolb's model of reflection (1974, 1975) and developed it into a more detailed and comprehensive overview of the process of reflection (Boud et al 1985: 20). Boud and colleagues remark that 'Kolb does not discuss the nature of his stage of observation and reflection in much detail ... his scheme has been useful in assisting us in planning learning activities [but] it does not help us, however, to uncover the elements of reflection itself'(Boud et al 1985: 13).

Jarvis (1987: 96), who had also used Kolb's model as a base for his own early work, saw Boud's work as offering the fullest discussion upon the process of reflection. Boud, Keogh and Walker (1985: 7-8) were convinced that, although drawing on previous experience was an important element of learning, there needed to be something to help individuals apply experiences in new contexts and derive maximum benefit from change in new situations. 'The more we thought about these issues, the more we identified the importance of what we termed "reflection"'. Boud et al saw reflection as having three characteristics (1985: 7):

1. Reflection is an act of each individual; teachers, coaches or counsellors only have access to whatever aspects of thoughts and feelings the individual chooses to reveal.
2. Reflection is purposeful; it does not refer to the meandering of the thought process; it is an act which is goal-directed and critical.

3. Reflection is a complex activity composed of both thoughts and emotions – positive and negative perceptions of the self. The fostering of a positive self-image is an important step towards transformative learning.

Boud and his colleagues acknowledge the influence of Dewey, Mezirow and Habermas in the development of their model and, like those authors, Boud et al considered that reflective learning had different, distinct stages (1985: 18-39). The first is where the individual recalls previous *experiences*. The authors see the use of written or verbal exercises as helpful in enabling the fullest recollection possible, not just at factual but also at emotional levels. The second stage seeks to recognize the *emotions and feelings* present in previous experiences, concentrating on the development of positive feeling. The third stage re-evaluates the experience in light of the *awareness* gained in first two stages. Boud et al see that, if each stage of the process is completed successfully, the outcome of the reflective process will offer new perspectives on experience, changes in behaviour, readiness for application and commitment to action.

   In more recent times Boud (Boud and Walker 1998; Boud 1999) has looked at the development of reflection and the impact of its increasing use in the design of educational programmes. Boud and Walker (1998: 191-197) have explored the most effective use of reflection on professional courses and conclude that, for a reflective approach to work, teachers need to take a sufficiently contextualised view of how they attempt to foster reflection. Taylor (1997: 11-12) also argues that adult learning literature has been remiss in discussing the context within which it operates, thus limiting its applicability to professional education. Boud and Walker further note that teachers espousing the reflective ideal need to be honest in confronting themselves, their processes and their outcomes. They recommend that such a self-appraisal should be undertaken with the help of their peers (Boud and Walker 1998: 205).

Summary

This review of the reflective literature reveals an interconnection and circularity between theorists on the ideal of reflection, fitting perhaps for a concept that is by its nature interconnected and circular. Most of the theorists discussed strive, in individual ways, to achieve levels of meta-learning and perspective transformation through acts of reflection.

   This chapter has attempted to demonstrate the individual contributions made by different theorists while also making links to similarities in their work. To avoid restating the many interconnections noted within this chapter, Figure 2.2 has been designed to show the sequence of the work discussed in this chapter. By so doing, the theories of reflection discussed in this chapter can be demonstrated to have a clear chronological progression. Figure 2.3 demonstrates in diagrammatic form the acknowledged inter-relationships and influences between these theorists discussed in this chapter. It demonstrates, above all, the influence of Dewey on subsequent reflective theorists. In reviewing the literature for this chapter it is clear that, with the exception of Freire, all the theorists discussed in this chapter have acknowledged Dewey's influence in their published works. This lack of reference to Dewey's work on the part of Freire may be explained by the fact that Freire neither read nor wrote in English.

This exploration of the work of different reflective theorists has been important in allowing me to develop my reflective teaching and learning model in a manner which appreciates a number of different but complementary approaches towards reflection. Individual theorists have also contributed in other ways to my design of a reflective teaching and learning model. Dewey's ideas of the nature of the practicum, and the reflective teacher/researcher's place within it, have been used in considering the most effective method of balancing such a dual role. Mezirow's levels of critical reflection proved useful in helping me to appreciate the levels of reflection which both teacher and professional student participants could be expected to reach. Mezirow's views on adult learning have also helped to me to devise different reflective teaching approaches best suited to a group of professional adult learners. Finally, Brookfield's unambiguous objectives for effective reflection in teaching what standards of reflectivity I should aim for within the model.

This chapter has set out, in some detail, the philosophies and models which lead to, and run in parallel with, Donald A. Schon's notion of the reflective practitioner and the action theories of Argyris and Schön. By doing so it demonstrates not only how other writers have affected the evolution of Schön's ideas, but this review also sets down the fundamental principles of reflection and the philosophical influences which inform the development of this reflective teaching and learning model.

Figure 2.2   Chronology of Reflection 1910-2002

1910 | John Dewey – 1916
Democracy and Education

1930 | John Dewey – 1933
How We Think

1950 | George Kelly – 1955   Chris Argyris – 1957
The Psychology of Personal Constructs   *Personality and Organization*

1960 | Michael Polanyi – 1967   Jürgen Habermas – 1968
The Tacit Dimension   *Knowledge and Human Interest*

1970 | Paulo Freire – 1972   Argyris and Schön – 1974
Pedagogy of the Oppressed   *Theory in Practice*

Jürgen Habermas – 1974   David Kolb – 1975
Theory and Practice   *Applied Theory of Experiential Learning*

1980 | Jack Mezirow – 1981   Jürgen Habermas – 1981
A Critical Theory of Learning and Education   *Theory of Communicative Action*

Donald A. Schon – 1983
The Reflective Practitioner

Boud et al – 1985
Reflection – Turning Experience into Learning

Donald A. Schön – 1987   Stephen Brookfield – 1988
Educating the Reflective Practitioner   *Developing Critical Thinkers*

1990 | Mezirow and Associates – 1990
Fostering Critical Reflection in Adulthood

Donald A. Schön et al – 1991   Jack Mezirow – 1991
The Reflective Turn   *Transformative Dimensions of Adult Learning*

Paulo Freire – 1996   Stephen Brookfield – 1995
Pedagogy of Hope   *Becoming a Critically Reflective Teacher*

Brookfield and Preskill – 1999
Discussion as a Way of Teaching

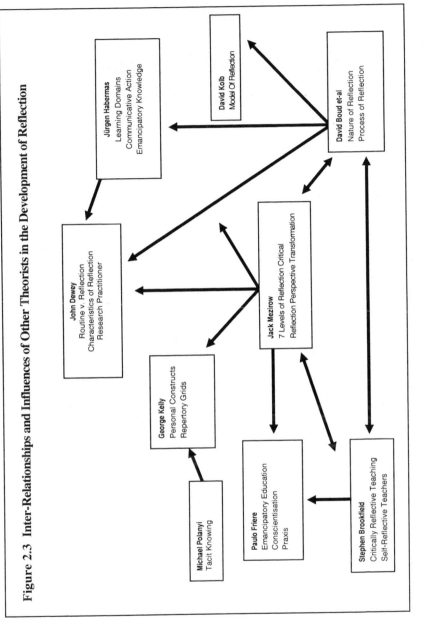

Figure 2.3 Inter-Relationships and Influences of Other Theorists in the Development of Reflection

*Arrows denote published acknowledgement of another theorist's work (i.e. makes reference to another's work)

Chapter 3

The Reflective Theories of
Argyris and Schön

As has been discussed in the previous chapter, the concept of reflection is far from new and has been developed in many directions by various authors. This gives rise to the potential risk that that the concept of reflection can lack coherence. Brookfield (1995: 216) cautions that one problem with the notion of reflective practice 'is that it has become a catch-all term embracing ideologies and orientations that are often contradictory'. Smyth (1992: 285) also warns that reflection 'runs the risk of being totally evacuated of all meaning'.

In the development of this model of reflective teaching and learning I have drawn on the work of a number of a number of theories of reflection and critical learning. However, the work of Schön and his collaborative work with co-author Chris Argyris is central to my approach to reflection and to my development of a reflective practicum where professionals can explore the fundamental nature of their work with clients. This decision to choose the work of particular theorists through which to develop a reflective approach stemmed partly from the need to settle on one particular definition of reflection upon which to centre my work. It also reveals the reality that, in the literature on reflection, Donald A. Schön emerges as a theorist of clarity and insight whose work has had relevance to practitioners in fields as diverse as nursing (Jarvis 1987, 1992; Powell 1989; Reed and Procter 1993); public planning and policy making (Bolan 1980; Forester 1980, 1991; Schön and Rein 1994); teaching and education (Mezirow et al 1990; Mezirow 1991; Jennings and Kennedy 1996; Brookfield 1995; Cranton 1994); music (Bamberger and Schön 1991; Lanzara 1991); organizational psychology and psychotherapy (Hirschhorn 1991; Gorell Barnes 1995); health services (Kember et al 2001) and social work (Yelloly and Henkel 1995; Gould 1989; Pray 1991; Papell and Skolnick 1992; Gould and Taylor 1996; Fook 1996, 2000; Fook et al 2002). The emergence of Schön's ideas and their application by authors such as these is shown in diagrammatic form at the end of this chapter (see Figure 3.9). This chapter begins with an exploration and a critical analysis of the work of Schön. It is then followed by a similar examination of the collaborative work of Argyris and Schön.

Schön

The term 'seminal' is frequently used in connection with Schön's writing (Jarvis 1992: 174, Gould 1996a: 2), particularly *The Reflective Practitioner* (Schön 1983) and its companion volume, *Educating the Reflective Practitioner* (Schön 1987). Perhaps one of the most important roles played by Schön's work is that it has had such relevance for such a variety of professionals, who have recognized it as a way to address the chronically difficult vacuum that exists between theory and practice.

It may not be coincidental that much interest in reflection in general and Schön's approach in particular, has come from professions which Nathan Glazer describes as 'minor, ones which cannot boast a strong epistemological grounding' (Glazer 1974: 346). These 'minor' professions are the same as those identified by Etzioni (1969) as 'semi-professions' – professions such as nursing, social work, planning, psychology and psychotherapy, which have long grappled with aspects of their practice that could not be easily reduced to fixed and testable scientific theory. Such minor professions contrast with the major 'learned' professions of medicine, law and engineering which are 'disciplined by an unambiguous end – health, success in litigation, profit – which settles men's minds' (Glazier 1974: 346). Schön (1983: 13-48) considered that the essence of professionalism had been consistently eroded by an over-emphasis on what he described as 'technically rational' views of professional training and practice, normally associated with the scientific major professions. This leads to a failure to recognize the unique qualities of practice competencies and professional artistry that also exists within professional practice. At the foundation of Schön's work (1992: 56-62) lies the argument that an alternative method of appreciating and fostering practice competencies is needed and that such a method should be based on the notion of reflection and reflective practice.

Schön's interpretation of reflection in practice acknowledged not only the inherent complexity and individuality of practice, it also offered a coherent model through which to appreciate practice skills and to develop them in a distinct, productive manner. Schön's own work, and his writing in collaboration with Chris Argyris, falls somewhere between purely theoretical works and the more descriptive, 'how-to' books of practical skills. As such, Schön's work attracts professionals who have found little inspiration in either 'camp' and who are also drawn to Schön's unambiguous and direct writing style which is illustrated by relevant case examples. This is not to suggest that Schön's writing lacks academic weight – it is held in high academic respect – but it also has an accessibility and clarity that appeals to many readers.

Schön's Impact on Different Professional Areas

Enthusiasm for Schön's work, and for his long-term collaboration with Chris Argyris, is to be found in the writing of many professionals seeking to adopt a more reflective approach to their practice. Schön's work is widely used in teacher education (Zeichner and Liston 1996: 14) where he is often referred to with the same respect as John Dewey. Argyris and Schön work is also to be found in journals of social work, sociology, nursing and medicine and in those of occupational therapy, human resource management, planning and design, technology management, curriculum development, disability studies, politics, psychology, public administration and sports studies (*Social Science Citation Index* 1995-2002).

It would be possible to review literature on reflective practice in any of the professional groups mentioned above and to find positive responses for Schön's ideas and his collaborative work with Argyris. In the field of nursing and nursing education, Burnard (1995a: 1167) notes that the notion of reflection and reflective practice has generated considerable interest and that the roots of such ideas are found in the work of Donald A. Schön. Greenwood (1998: 1183), in her critique of the work of Schön and his most frequent collaborator Chris Argyris says 'the contribution of these two scholars to the development of professional [nursing] education in the UK, Australia and North America has been enormous'. Powell (1989: 825), in her research on levels of reflection in nursing practice, found that, although reflection in relation to learning has been widely discussed, 'Schön's work gives a new dimension to the topic'. Finally, in the context of nursing, Jarvis (1992: 174), who has written extensively on refection and the nursing practitioner, acknowledges the influence of Habermas, Mezirow, Dewey and Freire. He also notes that by focusing on professions and professional practice Schön's work has raised so many new ideas about reflection.

Both theorists and practitioners in social work have found Schön's work offers them an important tool for bridging the theory/practice divide. Papell and Skolnick (1992: 20) consider that Schön's ideas fit well into the philosophical ethos underpinning social work. Other social work theorists have proposed that the use of Schön's model could address some difficulties in the value-stance of the profession. Pray (1991: 80) considers that traditional models of social work are based on practice assumptions that may constrain social workers from fully appreciating the individuality of those with whom they work. Pray notes that Schön's reflective model offers an alternative perspective which 'revitalizes the social worker's ability to truly honour and respect the uniqueness of each client'.

Not all writers have been so enthusiastic about the usefulness of Schön's model of reflective practice to social work. Ixer (1999: 513) considers that Schön's ideas lack practical application to social work, that they have been superseded by later theorists, and that Schön's entire oeuvre leaves more questions than answers. Ixer (1999: 519-520) argues that social work practitioners are unique in having to make swift, complex value judgements and that Schön's methodology does not take account of the serious consequences of delaying a decision in social work. While Papell and Skolnick (1992: 24) would not agree with Ixer's assertion that social work is unique in having to confront ethical and value dilemmas, they do consider that Schön does not extensively examine ethical considerations as an intrinsic part of his schema. However, Dominelli (1998: 10) suggests that the notion of self-knowledge is central to Schön's ideas on reflective practice and she sees self-knowledge as important in developing anti-oppressive social work practice.

Gould (1996a) considers that Schön's work allows for an examination of the relationship between theory and practice in social work in a unique and innovative way. He sees this as being particularly important at a time when 'British social work education ... has been pressured to accept a severe intellectual reductionism which treats everything from professional ethics to legal knowledge as "competencies" to be ticked off from a functional checklist' (Gould 1996a: 5). Working in an Australian context, Fook (1996: 6) sees that Schön's approach offers in concrete social work practice 'what has been argued for in theory for some time – the actual integration of theory, practice and research.' Lastly, Ming Tang (1998: 23-25) considers that a reflective approach allows social workers to become aware of the potential of their practice to become value laden. She argues that the desire to become self-reflective is indicative of a caring social worker who 'needs to be self-critical in assessing whether their practice is serving the best interests of service users and how it is affected by personal values, feeling and orientation' (1998: 25).

Development of Schön's Work

Schön's journey to reflective practice shows a long-standing interest in design – in physical, environmental and interpersonal contexts. Originally educated as a philosopher, Schön's work has been considerably influenced by John Dewey on whom he based his doctoral dissertation. In the early 1970s Schön took part in a study of architectural education (Schön 1971). As Schön says of this move, 'I did not anticipate the kind of intellectual journey I was in for' (Argyris and Schön 1996: xi). Working with a team from the Massachusetts Institute of Technology, he began studying the kind of knowledge that makes practitioners good at what they do. These studies, although originally based on architectural practice, expanded to embrace professions such as engineering, management, law, psychotherapy and city planning (Argyris and Schön 1996: xi).

In the 1970s Schön also began what was to be his most fruitful collaborative work with Chris Argyris. Argyris's earlier research (*Personality and Organization* (1957) and *Integrating the Individual and the Organization* (1964)) had focused on how individuals are affected by, and adapt to, formal organizational structures, executive leadership and management information systems. Argyris then moved to studying ways of changing organizations: *Interpersonal Competence and Organizational Effectiveness* (1962), *Organization and Innovation* (1965), looking especially at the behaviour of executives at the upper levels of organizations (Argyris 1982: xxvi).

Argyris and Schön began to develop a theory of individual and organizational learning in which human reasoning, not just behaviour, becomes the basis for diagnosis and action (1974, 1978). This collaborative work is important because Argyris and Schön's Model I and Model II framework, which they designed at that time, has been used to inform the 'full model rotation' phase of this reflective teaching model. Argyris and Schön continued their joint work for almost a quarter of a century and had published *Organizational Learning II* (1996), a long awaited follow-up to the original *Organizational Learning* (1974), less than a year before Schön's death in 1997.

In 1983 Schön published his most famous work, *The Reflective Practitioner*, in which he argued for a new epistemology of practice, one 'which would stand the question of professional knowledge on its head' (Schön 1987: xi). The book focused on the competence and artistry already imbedded in skilful practice. Schön proposed that such artistry was a far more relevant base for professional education than the 'technically rational', systematic, theory-based knowledge traditionally associated with university-based teaching methods. His companion volume to *The Reflective Practitioner* (1983), *Educating the Reflective Practitioner* (1987), drew out the implications of Schön's original ideas for the education of practitioners and for education in general (Argyris and Schön 1996: xi). Both books are marked by a refreshingly clear writing style and by the wide use of ideographic case examples. In the 1990s Schön edited a book of case studies of reflection in different educational settings, *The Reflective Turn* (1991) and, with Professor Martin Rein, he published *Frame Reflection* (1994) which examined reflection at policy level. Appropriately his last work was his 1996 collaboration with Chris Argyris, with whom he had shared 'many wonderful hours double-loop learning' (Argyris 1982).

Schön's Reflective Practitioner

Schön's basic hypothesis is that within the latter half of the twentieth century there has been a growing discontent with the nature of professionalism and with the nature of professional practice (Schön 1983, 1987, 1992).

> The crisis of confidence in the professions, and perhaps also the decline in professional self-image, seems to be rooted in a growing scepticism about professional effectiveness in the larger sense, a sceptical reassessment of the professions' actual contribution to society's well being through the delivery of competent services based on special knowledge (Schön 1983: 13).

He proposed that the origin of this discontent lay in the technically rational approach inherent in most professional education, research and supervision which is supported and enhanced by academic, theory-based education (1983: 40-48). Technical rationality only allows for a logical scientific explanation of reality in which 'scientific knowledge is the only knowledge real or worth having; analogue knowledge is non-existent or inferior and fact and value have nothing to do with each other' (Berman 1981: 233).

This reveals the core of what Schön regarded as the problem of how professional education and practice had evolved. He saw that most professionals gain their professional knowledge primarily through university-based, technically rational training. However, he also saw that this knowledge is too limited to deal with many of the complex problems that face most professionals in their everyday professional practice (Schön 1987: 10). Schön suggested that such a background produces professionals who may be incapable of either recognizing or valuing the seemingly intangible qualities of practice wisdom and that this has caused an artificial and profitless division between theory and practice. Thus the splitting of 'theory' and 'practice', with its inherent confusion and obstructions, has caused an unnatural divide for both professionals and their clients. In this regard, Schön proposed his most memorable and widely quoted analogy:

> In the varied topography of professional practice, there is a high hard ground where practitioners can make effective use of research-based theory and technique, and there is a swampy lowland where situations are incapable of technical solution. The difficulty is that the problems of the high ground, however great their technical interest, are often relatively unimportant to client or to the larger society, while in the swamp are the problems of the greatest human concern. Shall the practitioner stay on the high, hard ground where he can practice rigorously, as he understands rigor, but where he is constrained to deal with problems of relatively little social importance? Or will he descend to the swamp where he can engage the most important and challenging problems if he is willing to forsake technological rigor? (Schön 1983: 42)

This illustration of the dilemma of relevance or rigour in professional practice may well be the most quoted section of all the works of Donald A. Schön and, indeed, Schön restates this analogy in a number of his subsequent works (Schön 1987: 3, 1992: 52). Its popularity can be attributed to the fact that it sums up so well the philosophy of Schön and it also offers a rationale for his work in devising and developing his approach to reflective practice.

Returning to his analogy of the high ground and the swampy lowlands, Schön suggests that practitioners tend to favour one position or the other. The high-ground theorists may confine themselves to narrow technical practice where 'they pursue an agenda driven by evolving questions of modelling theory and techniques, increasingly divergent from the contexts of actual practice' (Schön 1992: 55). When such theoretical approaches do not work, practitioners may explain such failures by the use of terms such as 'patient resistance' and 'client non-compliance' and blame clients when they are dissatisfied with professional practice.

Practitioners 'in the swamp', however, immerse themselves in practice situations, relying on intuition to respond to each individual and frequently confusing, practice episodes. Schön argues that much of this intuitive practice produces innovative solutions to problems (1987: 12) but, because they occur in a frequently haphazard manner, little long-term constructive learning occurs that can be replicated in future similar situation. Lowland practitioners are, therefore, often regarded as being of a lower order than their technically rational counterparts and frequently feel inferior to them 'even those who choose the swamp tend to pay homage to prevailing models of rigor. What they know how to do, they have no way of describing as rigorous' (Schön 1992: 55).

Schön's work has examined the nature of professional practice and has developed new approaches to practice that capture and employ individual creativity, not as a chance occurrence, but as a basis of measurable and reproducible practice competence (1987: 13). Instead of practice being a lower-order manifestation of cleaner and tidier theory, it becomes, in Schön's hands, a combination of knowledge and action 'producing a sense of professional freedom and a connection with rather than a distance from clients' (Pietetroni 1995: 43).

Working in the Practicum

One of the unique characteristics of Schön's writing is his use of qualitative and ideographic case studies of practice in such diverse fields as engineering, town planning, psychoanalysis, architecture, music, psychotherapy and counselling (Schön 1983, 1987, 1991, Bamberger and Schön 1991). In these case studies Schön has examined the components of skilled practice and he has attempted to demonstrate the knowledge inherent in these spontaneous intuitive performances of action. Schön places this examination within what he terms a 'practicum', a place which simulates the conditions of practice, but which allows the practitioner space and time to appreciate the nuances and interconnections between theory, intuition and practice (Schön 1987: 36-40). Individuals who can do so are, in Schön's term 'reflective practitioners'.

In the practicum, a skilled coach works intensively on a piece of practice with a practitioner/students and the role of the reflective coach is central to Schön's notion of developing reflective practice. Here Schön demonstrates that such exploration of practice uncovers levels of knowledge and skill that are extra to, and separate from, the existing theories held by practitioners. He maintains that such practice knowledge tends to be mostly tacit and is difficult for the practitioner to recognize and appreciate. This is similar to Polanyi's 'tacit knowledge' (Polayni 1967) and Dewey's 'routine action' (1916: 77-78). However, Schön argues that such practice knowledge, or 'how to', rests at the base of most professional actions. This forms the basis of the first of Schön's milestones of reflective practice – the recognition of 'knowing-in-action' (Schön 1983: 49-54).

Knowing-In-Action

'Knowing-in-action' refers to the implicit knowledge that underpins and accompanies action, the characteristic mode of ordinary practical knowledge (Schön 1983: 54). Schön suggests that when such tacit knowledge produces surprising results, either good or bad, then an opportunity occurs for the practitioner to reflect on action that has been, up to this point, automatic and spontaneous. This reflection may occur within the action itself, leading to 'reflection-in-action', or subsequent to the action, in reflection-on-action. Schön

(1992: 56-58) argues that this awareness and development of practice is far more than trial and error behaviour and, especially when facilitated within the practice, becomes a unique and skilled learning process. The steps leading from 'knowing-in-action' to reflection have been described by Schön in a number of his works (1983: 49-69; 1992: 58) and they have been amalgamated and developed further in Figure 3.1.

Figure 3.1   Schön's Process of Reflective Practice

KNOWING-IN-ACTION
In the context of the performance of some task, the performer spontaneously initiates a routine of action, which produces an unexpected routine.

⇩

SURPRISE RESULT
The performer notices the unexpected result which he construes as surprise – an error to be corrected, an anomaly to be made sense of, an opportunity to be exploited.

⇩

KNOWLEDGE-IN-ACTION
Surprise triggers reflection, directed both to the surprising outcome and to the knowing-in-action that led to it. It is although the performer asked himself, 'What is this?' and at the same time, 'What understandings and strategies of mine have led me to produce this?'

⇩

REFLECTION-ON-ACTION
The performer restructures his understanding of the situation – his framing of the problem he has been trying to solve, his picture of what is going on, or his strategy of action he has been employing.

⇩

REFLECTION-IN-ACTION
On the basis of this restructuring, he invents a new strategy of action.

⇩

REFLECTIVE PRACTICE
He tries out the new action he has invented, running an on-the-spot experiment whose results he interprets, in turn, as a 'solution', an outcome on the whole satisfactory, or else as a new surprise that calls for a new round of reflection and experimentation.

Adapted from Schön (1983:49-69, 1992:58)

What is important to note is that the learning engendered in reflective practice is not merely trial-and-error. The reflective practitioner needs to make this learning explicit, where 'the process has a form, an inner logic according to which reflection on the unexpected consequences of one action influence the design of the next one' (Schön 1992: 58). Schön considered that when someone reflects in action, he becomes a researcher in the practice context, not dependent on the categories of established theory and technique, but able to construct a new theory of the unique case (Schön 1983: 68). This explicit learning may be done by the individual or be facilitated by a reflective coach within the practicum.

Reflective Practice and Reflective Coaching

Schön argued that mastery in performance is highly prized, seldom quantified and rarely taught in a constructive manner (1987: 211). His work seeks to investigate the levels of reflection-in-action essential to the development of professional artistry and to recognize and incorporate such competence in professional development. He sees that 'just as some people learn to reflect-in-action, so do others learn to help them to do so', and he classifies those 'rare individuals not so much as teachers but coaches of reflection-in-action' (Schön 1992: 62).

Schön's practicum allows for the establishment of a coaching environment that recognizes and fosters competence not just as an adjunct to theory but as a phenomenon which is of equal importance in the development and training of new professionals. Schön's view of the role of the reflective coach has been influential in the coaching role adopted by me in this research. Schön (1992: 62) also emphasized the need for such coaches to develop their own personal artistry and reflection within the teaching process. This echoes Brookfield's view of critically reflective teachers who must be 'open to rethinking their own commitments and the accuracy of the assumptions on which those commitments are founded' (1995: 256). As has been examined in the previous chapter, much of Schön's rationale for the use of the practicum and the reflective coach is derived from the work of John Dewey. Schön (1987: 17) cites Dewey's insistence that the student needs not to be taught, but to be coached. 'He has to see on his own behalf and in his own way the relations between means and methods employed and results achieved. Nobody else can see for him, and he can't see just by being 'told', although the right kind of telling may guide his seeing and thus help him to see what he needs to see' (Dewey 1974: 151). It is this dual role of reflective practitioner and reflective coach that initially attracted me to Schön's work. As a practitioner and a teacher, Schön's work seemed to offer me an opportunity not only to examine and develop my own artistry within my teaching practice; it also offered a way that allowed for the transmission of such skills in a coherent and meaningful way with students.

Reflective Practice and Professionalism

Schön hypothesized that, if professionals begin to reflect upon their practice they can then use the knowledge gained from that reflection to develop and improve their practice, making it more responsive to their clients' needs. Simply put, once professionals begin to think about what they are doing, they are less likely to produce habitual professional responses that may have little to do with their clients' unique and complex needs. The traditional professional-client contract is based upon the professional having specific expertise that they agree to deliver to the client. The client in turn agrees to accept the professional's authority in his special field and to submit to the professional's ministrations (Schön 1983: 292). It is fair to admit that, although ultimately unproductive, the role of the authoritative expert has a good deal of personal kudos and adulation attached to it. However, Schön notes that as the professional moves towards new reflective competencies, he gives up some familiar sources of satisfaction and opens himself to new ones. Figure 3.2. shows how the two stances can be perceived from the point of view of the professional.

Figure 3.2   Model I/Model II Practitioner Perspectives

Expert	Reflective Practitioner
I am presumed to know and must do so, regardless of my own uncertainty.	I am presumed to know, but I am not the only one with relevant knowledge. My uncertainty may be a source of learning for me and for others.
Keep my distance from the client; hold on to the 'expert' role. Give the client a sense of my expertise, but convey a feeling of warmth and sympathy as a 'sweetener'.	Seek out connections with client's thoughts and feelings. Allow client to develop respect for my knowledge from its evidence in our working relationship.
Look for deference and status in the client's response to my professional persona.	Look for sense of freedom and of real connection with client. A professional 'facade' is no longer a necessity.
	Schön (1983: 300)

Such a shift in the nature of professionalism is also disquieting for the client. Moroney cautions that clients may be frustrated by the reflective practitioner for this reason. Clients 'have been socialized into a role of having faith in professionals and wanting them to guarantee security, being unquestioningly compliant and expecting unerring professional expertise and caregiving' (Moroney et al 1998: 43). Schön acknowledges this problem, but points out that it is principally this unrealizable expectation of professionals which has led to the crisis of confidence in professional knowledge in the first place. He warns that just as the reflective practitioner must give up the expert model, so the client must 'distance himself from his own attraction to the professional mystique' (Schön 1983: 300) Fig 3.3 demonstrates differing client perspectives in this regard.

Figure 3.3   Model I/Model II Client Perspectives

Traditional Contract Model I	Reflective Contract Model II
I put myself in the professional's hands. In doing this I gain a sense of security based on faith.	I join with the professional in making sense of my case. I gain a sense of increased involvement and action.
I have the comfort of being in good hands. I will comply with the advice offered and all will be well. I need only comply with his advice and all will be well.	I can exercise some control over the situation. I am not wholly dependent on the professional – he is also dependent on my information and actions.
I am pleased to be served by the best person available.	I am pleased to be able to test my judgements about the professional's competence. I enjoy discovering his knowledge, the phenomena of his practice and also discovering about myself. Schön (1983: 302)

Critique of Schön's Theory of Reflective Practice

Links with Other Theorists   In reviewing the literature of those who have written about Schön, it is far easier to find supporters rather than critics. However, there are aspects of Schön's work that remain problematic. The first of these is Schön's lack of acknowledgement of other contemporary theorists working in similar areas. I have already noted Schön's lack of acknowledgement of Habermas's work on emancipatory learning; neither does he refer to Mezirow's writing on perspective transformation, even in his later works (Schön 1991, 1992). Gould (1989: 14) also contends that there are striking parallels between Schön's epistemology of practice and George Kelly's view of the person as scientist; again this is not admitted by Schön. Lastly, Eraut (1995: 21) notes that, in an overall sense, Schön fails to link his analysis to the work of other researchers in the field. This failure to make connections between him and other contemporary theorists is frustrating, as it limits the ability to place his work in a wider contextual framework. It is unlikely that Schön was unaware of the work of theorists such as Habermas and Mezirow. I would argue that Schön's work probably reached its zenith with the publication of his 1983 *The Reflective Practitioner* and that much of his later work tended to be a re-statement of some of those ideas. This is evidenced in Schön's tendency to repeat sections of his work verbatim,[1] a practice not unknown in academic circles, but somewhat surprising for a theorist of Schön's calibre.

Mysterious Expertise   Schön's theory of the reflective practitioner is not without its difficulties. Schön is adept at describing the importance of developing tacit, implicit practice into thoughtful reflective practice. However, he is not as explicit in describing how this change is actually going to take place. Schön argues (1983: 304-305) that the technically rational 'expert' professional uses a cloak of 'mystery' in his practice, which serves to distance his client and to enhance his expert demeanour. Schön insists that this professional mystery must be dispelled before the client can experience a real connection with the professional. It can be argued that in Schön's case studies (1983, 1987), his reflective coaches still retain a degree of professional mystery in their own work. The case studies reveal how, in the hands of a reflective coach, the professionals whose work is being explored, are changing their perspectives on that work. However, Schön seldom discloses *how* the reflective coach is attempting to achieve this perspective change or if the coach himself is experiencing reflection-in-action. This results in seeing the benefits of increasing reflectivity on the part of the professionals, but an inability to be sure how it has happened. Thus Schön, while asking his readers to appreciate the swampy lowland, may allow his coaches to retain a foothold on the stony high ground.

Reflection and Educational Oppression Ixer (1999: 520-521) posits a related point when he suggests that professional educators, who are attempting to assess the reflective characteristics of students, could be behaving in an educationally oppressive manner. Ixer's suggestion is that, in requiring students to be reflective, teachers could abuse the power of their position with students. Ixer's assumption that professional educators will unquestionably perceive the ability to reflect, as an assessable competence, is debatable in itself. However, it does highlight the danger

---

[1] For example, Schön reproduces, verbatim, a 20-page section of The *Reflective Practitioner* (1983: 79-103) in *Educating the Reflective Practitioner* (1987: 44-65). He also reproduces a lengthy paragraph describing the dilemma of rigour or relevance, verbatim, in four separate publications (1983: 42, 1987: 3, 1992: 54, 1995: 28).

of a reflective approach being applied by teachers who are not reflective in themselves, a point which Schön fails to explore in any great detail.

Having considered the foregoing difficulties inherent in some of Schön's work I consider that he still advances a theory that is relevant for training practitioners to develop thoughtfulness and responsiveness in their work. Schön's arguments in relation to the problems of the technically rational practitioner are compelling and his clear vision of the role of the reflective practitioner has a clarity and cogency which appeals to a huge number of practitioners from different backgrounds. Peterson (1995: 98) saw that Schön, well aware of the danger and discomfort that lay before him, chose to leave the high ground of technical rationality for the complex and confusing swamp of practice, 'while never considering it necessary to fly off into an intuitive never-neverland'. Having explored Schön's theory of reflection, this chapter will now move to his collaborative work with Argyris (1974, 1996). The genus of this work pre-dates Schön's individual exploration of reflection, but many of Schön's ideas on reflective practice are evident in the collaborative writing.

Argyris and Schön's Theories of Action

Argyris and Schön's collaborative work on theories of action dates from 1971 when they were asked to help to train educational administrators to design and implement programmes of reform within second-level schools in the United States of America. They were to consider the types of skills that these administrators would need in order to be effective and what experience would help them acquire such skills. This task led Argyris and Schön to consider how skills, which they called 'theories of action', were acquired. They also examined how such acquisition was helped or hindered by the existing beliefs and models which individuals already hold and which already determine their practice. In their 1974 *Theory in Practice,* Argyris and Schön examined the issues of identifying the pre-existing beliefs and theories held by individuals and the necessity of acknowledging and challenging such beliefs before the development of new theories can occur.

Espoused Theory and Theory-in-use

The difference between what we say we do (espoused theory) and what we actually end up doing (theory-in-use) is central to Argyris and Schön's work. 'When someone is asked how he would behave in certain circumstances, the answer he usually gives is his espoused theory of action for that situation. This is the theory of action to which he gives allegiance and which, upon request, he communicates to others' (Argyris and Schön 1974: 6). In contrast to the espoused theory, the action that an individual will actually perform (his/her theory-in-use) may differ substantially from his espoused theory: 'the theory which actually governs his actions is his theory-in-use, which may or may not be compatible with his espoused theory; furthermore, the individual may or may not be aware of the incompatibility (Argyris and Schön 1974: 7) It is not only the difference between the espoused theory and the theory-in-use which is stressed in Argyris and Schön's work, but also the ways in which individuals can be made aware of these differences in their own work. This leads to what Mezirow et al consider emancipatory learning (Mezirow et al 1990: xv) and the subsequent creation of what Schön went on to name 'reflective practice' (1983).

Argyris and Schön saw theory-in-use as being both the means of getting what an individual wants – resolution of conflict, closing a deal, making a living – and also as a way of maintaining a degree of consistency which imposes boundaries on behaviour (Argyris and Schön 1974: 15). For example, one may want to achieve an end result and one's actions will be focused on that goal. One's actions (informed by a theory-in-use) will, however, also be limited by desires to keep other variables such as expense, personal stress and self-esteem within acceptable personal limits. Argyris and Schön argue that the individual desire to control variables within constant limits causes special conflict:

> when our theories-in-use prove ineffective in maintaining the constancy of our governing variables, we may find it necessary to change our theories-in-use. But we try and avoid such change because we wish to keep our theory-in-use constant. Forced to choose between getting what we want and maintaining second order consistency, we may choose not to get what we want (Argyris and Schön 1974: 17).

The significant summation of this argument is that the individual's desire to continue behaving in a certain way may outweigh his/her disappointment at such behaviour not achieving a desired goal.

Single- and Double-loop Learning

Such conflicts demonstrate the differences between single-loop and double-loop learning (Ashby 1960, Argyris and Schön 1974: 18-19). Single-loop learning refers to the acquisition of enough skills to maintain an existing situation, whereas double-loop learning allows for a critical appraisal of the existing situation and, if this found to be defective, new skills to set new goals and behaviours need to be acquired in order to achieve these goals.

An example of theory-in-action could be seen in a scenario of classroom management. Here, in order to maximize her students' potential for learning, a teacher may feel it imperative to create a classroom environment that would be as free from distractions as possible – this would be her espoused theory. To achieve this situation, she might strive to keep the classroom very much under her control and to teach in such a way as to minimize student interruption – this represents her theory-in-use. Despite her best efforts her students become restless and bored – she now has two courses of action open to her. In single-loop learning the teacher will strive to learn more skills to further increase class control but will not address the fundamental problem that her theory-in-use is not working. She may, alternatively, consider that maintaining such strict control is, in fact, detrimental to the learning process of the students and ultimately to her own effectiveness as a teacher. If she does so, she may now strive to acquire skills that allow for the development of more inclusive teaching styles, greater student involvement and a deepening of the learning experience. Such a response can be seen as double-loop learning – learning that the original theory-in-use was ineffective and then acquiring skills to modify the theory-in-use to bring it more in line with the espoused theory.

> Single-loop learning enables us to avoid continuing investment in the highly predictable activities that make up the bulk of our lives; but the theory-builder becomes a prisoner of his programs if he allows them to continue unexamined indefinitely. Double-loop learning changes the governing variables of one's programs and causes ripples to fan out over one's whole system of theory-in-use (Argyris and Schön 1974: 19).

The importance of evaluating theories-of-action and differentiating between espoused theories and theories-in-use is central to the work of Argyris and Schön. They stress that the less public testing of assumptions about a theory in use, the more likely the entire process will become self-sealing. In the classroom example, one of the main factors which moves the individual from single-loop learning (which maintains the faulty theory-in-use), to double-loop, or emancipatory learning, is the seeking of feedback, the public testing of personal assumptions. The teacher who continues to increase classroom control is unlikely to seek feedback, whereas the teacher who changes her theory-in-use is far more likely to seek feedback from both students and colleagues when she runs into problems. The following diagram (Figure 3.4) demonstrates Argyris and Schön's partialisation of action theory, using the above example of classroom control. This model of a theory of action has been used as the basis of an analytic tool in this reflective teaching and learning model.

Model I and Model II Practice

Figure 3.4 also demonstrates an important theme in the work of Argyris and Schön – the concept of Model I and Model II practice. Argyris and Schön's definition of Model I and Model II practice would have strong parallels, respectively, with Schön's technically rational, expert practice and his reflective practice. A large part of Argyris and Schön's collaborative work since the early 1970s has been, through an action research methodology, to examine the theories-in-use of over five thousand individuals (1992: xxii). This includes an analysis of Model I or Model II practice tendencies in the professionals being studied.

Argyris and Schön's method of collecting data for such analysis was to ask individual practitioners to reproduce, on paper, a challenging incident in their work.

Figure 3.4   Argyris and Schön's Theory of Action

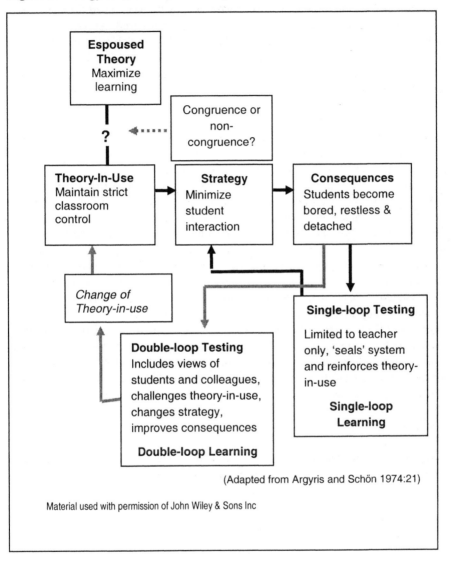

(Adapted from Argyris and Schön 1974:21)

This incident was expressed at an external level, reproducing the dialogue that had occurred and also at an internal level where the practitioners noted their unspoken emotions during the interaction. By examining this material, Argyris and Schön asked respondents to make explicit the governing variables and subsequent strategies of action that determined their behaviour (1974: 42-43). As Putnam states, the results of this research suggested that 'virtually everyone acts consistently with the theories-in-use which Argyris and Schön call Model I' (1992: 146).

As part of my reflective teaching and learning model, I wanted to use the concepts inherent in this analysis of a theory of action as part of a self-administered audit that students could use to explore incidents from their own practice. Argyris and Schön's technique of diagnosing theories-in-use, as shown above (Figure 3.4), is complex in both its shape and in the language it uses. Suspecting that this might be the case, I attempted to use Argyris and Schön's ideas of theory of action in this form with a number of groups. I discovered that a majority of the students had difficulties with both the linguistic and structural complexities of the framework. Because of this, in my use of the theory of action within the full model rotation phase of my reflective teaching and learning model, I chose to simplify both its language and its outline to facilitate its use by students. My simplified theory of action analysis technique, called the Four-Question Case Audit was designed to be administered by students themselves so that they could assess the extent of Model I and Model II variables in their own practice. This differs from Argyris and Schön's technique for diagnosing theory-in-use that was not intended to be shared with the participants, but was only used as a diagnostic tool by the researchers. The results of the application of the Four-Question Case Audit (4.Q.C.A.) on the professional students' case studies are fully documented in Chapter 7.

Model I

Argyris and Schön found four consistent governing variables used by professionals whose practice could be described as predominately Model I:

- achievement of goals unilaterally defined by the practitioner
- a maximization of winning and a minimization of losing
- suppression of negative expressions of feelings
- the need to be rational (Argyris and Schön 1974: 63-95).

The authors go on to demonstrate how such governing variables in Model I produce action strategies and consequences which lead on to self-sealing, single-loop learning situations with little or no public testing of assumptions and an ultimate decrease in personal effectiveness. Argyris and Schön produced a number of outlines of Model I and Model II behaviours (Argyris and Schön 1974: 66-87; Argyris and Schön 1978: 62-63 and 136-137; Schön 1987: 256-259; Argyris and

Schön 1996: 93 and 118) and Figures 3.5 and 3.6 show an amalgamation of these ideas.

Figure 3.5   Model I Theory-In-Use

Governing variables	Action strategies	External consequences	Learning consequences
Define goal and how to achieve them	Design and manage environment	Individual seen as defensive, competitive, controlling	Self-sealing No learning
Maximize winning and minimize losing	Own and control tasks	Defensive interpersonal and group relationships	Single-loop learning
Minimize generating or expressing negative feelings	Protect yourself Blame others, create stereotypes, intellectualize	Risk-taking is limited, power-centred competition, rivalry and suspicion is high	Little public testing – much private testing of theories
Be rational and minimize expression of emotion	Avoid confrontations, censor information, hold private meetings	Freedom of information or choice is reduced	

Adapted from Argyris and Schön (1974: 66-87), Argyris and Schön (1978: 62-63 and 136-137), Schön (1987: 256-259), Argyris and Schön (1996: 93 and 118)

In their last joint publication Argyris and Schön (1996: xxiii-xxiv) defended the continuing viability of their ideas of Model I and Model II practice. They noted that the consequences for the governing variable and action strategies of Model I have increasing resonance in a world governed by defensiveness, escalating demands on the individual and a decreasing tolerance of failure at any level. Their research over a twenty-year period reveals that the overwhelming majority of practitioners adopt Model I theories-in-use in threatening or embarrassing situations. In such environments, 'strength becomes defined in terms of winning, maintaining unilateral control of situations and keeping private one's own feelings of vulnerability' (Argyris and Schön 1996: 96).

Model II

If Argyris and Schön's Model I is basically a theory of unilateral control over others, their Model II proposes a theory of shared control and equity. Argyris and

Schön's Model II has, as its governing variables, a commitment to valid information, free and informed choice and a pledge to open monitoring of the interaction. By setting such variables the authors suggest that an individual adopting a Model II position will be viewed as less defensive and open to the opinions and ideas of others (see Figure 3.6). Model II practitioners still hold their own views but show a willingness to publicly test out the validity of their opinions, to confront inconsistencies between their espoused theories and their theories-in-use and to be willing to change. An important factor in Model II behaviour is that, with an easing of defensiveness, a much higher level of reflective learning can be expected. Such a hypothesis concurs with Habermas's domain of emancipatory learning (1971: 310), Freire's stage of critical consciousness (1972: 85-87) and, most strongly, with Mezirow's level critical reflection (1990: 6). Argyris and Schön see this learning as being of benefit to all individuals in the interaction.

> As individuals feel higher degrees of freedom of choice, trust and authenticity they are more likely to test their assumptions publicly, which is likely to enable others to feel higher degrees of freedom of choice, trust and authenticity – all of which makes everyone more willing to give valid information that enables individuals to test their assumptions (Argyris and Schön 1974: 92).

This indicates that the authors hope that Model II behaviour will beget Model II behaviour and that the subsequent double-loop learning allows for changes in governing variables and task re-definition which will be productive and energizing.

It would be easy to see Model II as the antithesis of Model I, but they do not represent polar opposites. Instead, they can be seen as two routes to the same end. In both models the practitioner strives to achieve a specified goal and it is important to remember that both Model I and Model II practitioners can be equally sincere in their wish to bring about the best possible changes both for themselves and for their clients. What is different about Model I practitioners are their use of underlying unilateral controls which sanction the use of defensive reasoning (Argyris and Schön 1996: 107). Model I behaviour, as perceived by Argyris and Schön, is fixed, controlled and resistant to change, despite indications that it may not be productive. This being so, Model I practitioners could unequivocally claim that their actions are far from controlling while, at the same time, utilizing defensive mechanisms so entrenched that they themselves are unaware of their effectiveness. Anderson makes a interesting point in this regard, she sees the defensive behaviour inherent in Model I as being driven by a need to move away from something 'usually some truth about ourselves' (Anderson 1994: 7). Therefore, the move to Model II requires an awareness of such personal defensiveness and of the win/lose mind-set which encourages it. It is only by doing so that it becomes possible to confront basic assumptions, publicly test hypotheses and encourage personal growth and learning (Argyris and Schön 1974: 101).

Figure 3.6   Model II Theory-In-Use

Governing variables	Action strategies	External consequences	Learning consequences
Information is open and shared	Environment created over which participants feel they have some contribution and control	Individual seen as minimally defensive, a choice creator, a facilitator	Process open to evaluation and change. Learning sense as positive and energizing
Free and Informed Choice	Tasks are jointly controlled	Minimally defensive interpersonal and group relationships	Double-loop learning
Internal commitment to choice and open monitoring of its implementation	Protection of self is part of open, constructive collaborative process. Clear speech, watch own inconsistencies	Learning seen as important, open confrontation on difficult issues, individuality fostered	Theories are publicly tested

Problem solving encouraged |
| Open and constructive expression of emotion | Transparency in information giving, increased opportunities for sharing of ideas | Openness regarded as a norm, trust established and cherished | Learning is shared |

Adapted from Argyris and Schön (1974: 66-87), Argyris and Schön (1978: 62-63 and 136-137), Schön (1987: 256-259), Argyris and Schön (1996: 93 and 118)

Social Values of Model I and Model II Practice

Argyris and Schön, in their final publication (1996), also offered a new insight into Model I and Model II approaches in regard to their 'social value' – characteristics which are highly valued, such as respect for others, strength, honesty and integrity. The authors (1996: 119-121) point out that such prized values can exist quite happily in Model I practice and, indeed, can be used as a justification for the continuation of a Model I stance. However, such virtues in a Model I context may serve to exacerbate the unilateral control of situations. As Schön has describes, a technically rational or Model I professional may well 'use sympathy and warmth as a sweetener' in order to achieve her own ends (Schön 1983: 300).

What may well occur is that the Model II practitioner will appear less 'nice' or 'caring' than the Model I counterpart. Because of this he/she may, initially, not necessarily exude an air of comforting capability and expertise. Therefore, in a society that values the polite, nice expert, the decision for a professional to move towards Model II is not without difficulty or risk. This point is significant for the work undertaken by the professional students using my model. As will be discussed later in this book, a number of these students experienced discomfort in their attempts to increase the Model II component in their own practice. A further aspect of this discomfort was the realization that some of the organizations in which they work are, by their nature, Model I systems, which value and encourage Model I practice in the professional (Redmond 2003).

Argyris's individual work has also looked at the problems of the Model I organization in terms of organizational action (1982, 1994). His work indicates that many organizational systems, both physically and culturally, may be intrinsically Model I, thereby strongly encouraging and rewarding individual Model I behaviour. When limited personal learning occurs using a Model I approach, little notice will be taken by the larger Model I system, thereby ensuring its continuance at both micro and macro levels (Argyris and Schön 1996: xiii). In a way it is possible to see that, out of their theory of action, Argyris has focused on implementing change at macro, organization and managerial levels, while Schön has developed a more individualistic perspective, looking at developing Model II behaviour in the professional whom he terms the reflective practitioner.

Critique of Argyris and Schön's Theory of Action

While Schön's individual work is widely explored and acknowledged in the reflective literature, less interest is paid to his collaborative work with Argyris on theory of action. This may be due to the fact that their joint work is considered to be of more relevance to the area of organizational management, a view that may limit its usefulness in a wider area. One of the strengths of Argyris's and Schön's theory of action framework is that it offers a defined method of facilitating a group examination of dilemmas, values, beliefs and assumptions (Mezirow 1990a: 31). As such it is a more tangible and practical theory to apply in a practice situation than Schön's theory of reflective practice. Fook (1996: 3) notes that it was not until she began designing class exercises around Argyris and Schön's framework that she saw her work as specifically reflective. Ryan (1996: 112) also used the framework in a longitudinal study to help him monitor the development of his own performance as a researcher over the five-year period of a longitudinal study into the professional formation of social workers.

As I had noted in my preliminary work on this reflective model, Argyris and Schön's action theory framework can be quite complex if unquestioningly replicated in an unequivocal manner. Sadique (1996: 24), who describes herself as having been 'fascinated' by Argyris and Schön's framework, used their theory of action in her own research on social work competencies and found, in hindsight, that it overly complicated her research design. This is not only because the framework is complex in itself; it is also because Argyris and Schön have designed it to be part of the reflective coach's repertoire of skills. It is important to note that Argyris and Schön suggest that an individual is unable to diagnose his own theory-in-use: 'we cannot learn what someone's theory-in-use is simply by asking him. We must construct his theory-in-use from observation of his behaviour' (Argyris and Schön 1974: 7). In this way Argyris and Schön's joint work also reveals the same tendency as Schön to assume the reflective coach's mastery over the individual's ability to be reflective. I was keen to create an environment where the individuals could be facilitated to discover, for themselves, what their theory-in-use might be. In order to achieve this I designed, in the form of the Four-Question Case Audit (discussed in the next chapter), a diagnostic framework that goes beyond Argyris and Schön's technique where diagnosis is limited to the reflective coach. Instead, the Four-Question Case Audit provides participants with a diagnostic tool which they can understand and utilize themselves and which will offer them a method of diagnosing their own theories-in-use both within the practicum and also afterwards in their own practice settings.

Jarvis (1987: 93) sees Argyris and Schön's work as being important in demonstrating how people do not act in accordance with their reasoning and how they 'distance' themselves from the recognition of such incongruence. Jarvis (1987: 94) also comments that while Argyris and Schön explore how such behaviour can be ameliorated within an organization, they do not comment on the learning process, as such. While I recognize this limitation to Argyris and Schön's work and agree that their theories do not represent a full reflective methodology that is easily replicated in the classroom, Argyris and Schön's action theory does provide a sound framework upon which to begin to design new approaches to practice.

Summary

This chapter has looked at both the individual work of Schön on reflective practice and his collaborative work with Argyris on action theory. I have found that both strands of work have strengths and weaknesses. However, when explored together the two separate bodies of work prove complementary to each other. Taken on its own, Schön's work on reflective practice offers a challenging vision of a new professionalism without the finer details necessary to fully comprehend how it can be achieved. However, when studied in tandem with Argyris and Schön's theory of action, it is possible to see new perspectives of the reflective practitioner and to see how, in practical terms, reflective practice can be developed.

This chapter has also revealed connections between the work of Schön's and Argyris and the 'phases' of reflection already identified in the work of other theorists. Figure 3.7 demonstrates the comparison of these phases with those already identified. In the next chapter this grid of reflective phases is used as a basis upon which to construct the phases of a new reflective teaching model. In order to place the foregoing discussion of the work of Argyris and Schön into a wider perspective, Figure 3.8 offers a diagrammatic exploration of how the individual work of Schön and the theories of Argyris and Schön have developed and evolved, by looking at the thematic influences emerging from their work. This diagram also looks at how other theorists have incorporated Argyris and Schön's ideas into their own work.

In order to address the interactions that transpire between professionals and those with whom they work, it is necessary to acknowledge the complexities of such interactions, the different levels of communication which exist and the underlying motivations which exist within the interaction. In this quest for understanding, the work of Argyris and Schön (1974, 1996) offers a tested method of working with professionals which allows for the intricacies of the professional interaction to be disassembled. Genuine learning can then occur within that process: planned change can be both implemented and appraised. It is important to note Gould's caution that reflection is not, and by its nature can never be, a fixed process. Indeed, it is the very nature of reflective practice and reflective research that the application of Argyris and Schön's ideas must bring new insights and changes. 'If reflective learning is to be a dynamic influence then the theory has to be seen as reflexive, being itself transformed by the process of educators using the ideas and learning from that experience' (Gould 1996a: 5). It is in just such a spirit that I have drawn from the work of Argyris and Schön, seeing it as an important influence on my own reflective journey, while allowing me to develop and evolve this model of reflective teaching practice.

Figure 3.7 Comparison of Stages of Reflective Learning II

	Habitual action	New data to inform situation	Intellectualisation of problem / Formulation of new hypothesis	Testing of new hypothesis	Reflection and evaluation of hypotheses
Dewey	Habitual action	New data to inform situation	Intellectualisation of problem / Formulation of new hypothesis	Testing of new hypothesis	Reflection and evaluation of hypotheses
Mezirow	Unresolved dilemma based on habitual assumption	Trigger event	Perspective transformation	Emancipatory learning	Reflection on transformation
Habermas	Technical practice / Objectified processes	Exposure to new ideologies	Reassessment of previous meanings	Emancipatory learning domain	Emancipatory learning with self-reflection
Brookfield	Habitual working practices	Trigger event	Discomfort, exploration of old working practices	Development of alternative perspectives	Integration of new approaches
Argyris and Schön	Tacit knowledge	Inconsistencies in practice exposed	Knowledge-on-action	Reflection-on-action and reflection-in-action / Double-loop learning	Critical reflection

Figure 3.8 Thematic Influences of Argyris and Schön

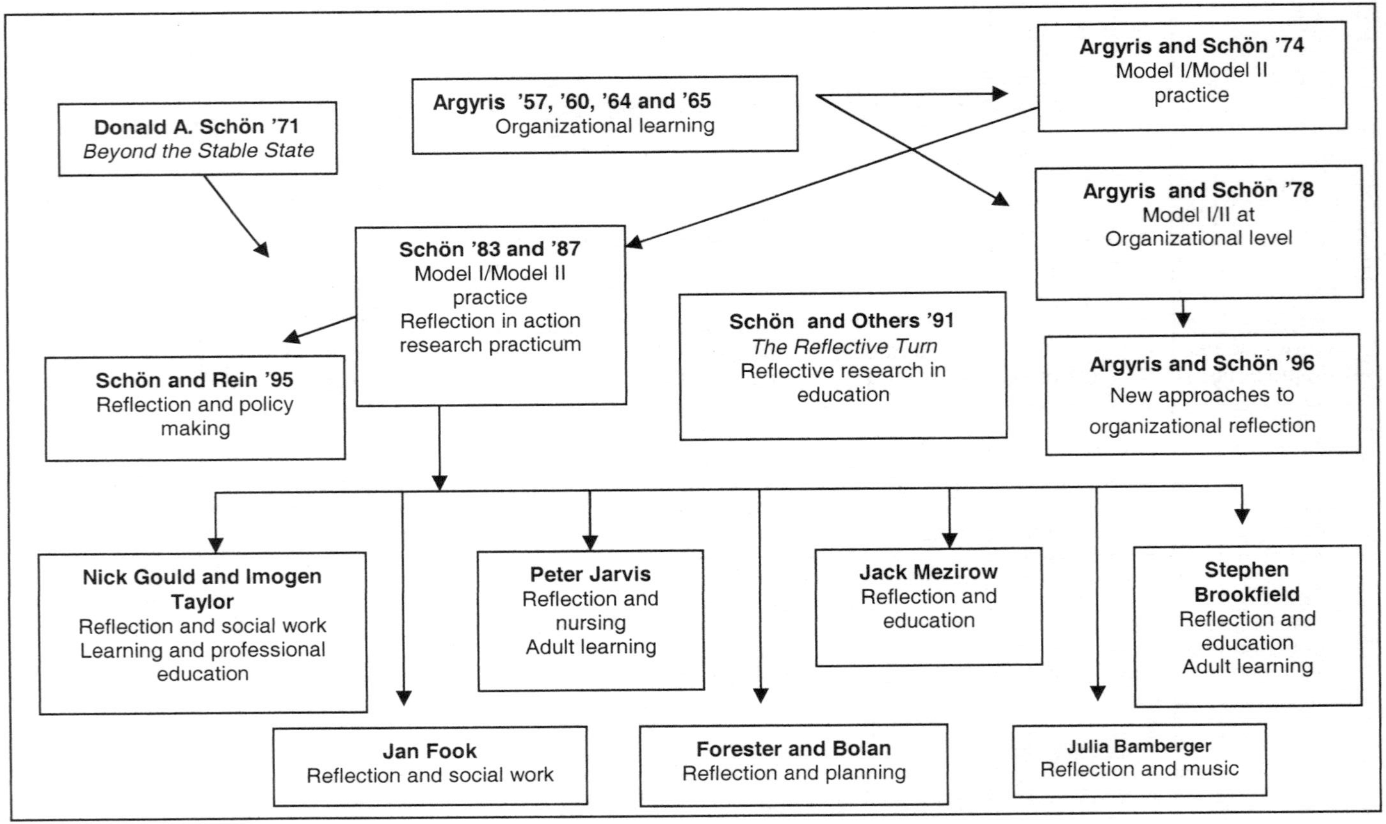

Donald A. Schön '71
Beyond the Stable State

Argyris '57, '60, '64 and '65
Organizational learning

Argyris and Schön '74
Model I/Model II
practice

Argyris and Schön '78
Model I/II at
Organizational level

Argyris and Schön '96
New approaches to
organizational reflection

Schön '83 and '87
Model I/Model II
practice
Reflection in action
research practicum

Schön and Others '91
The Reflective Turn
Reflective research in
education

Schön and Rein '95
Reflection and policy
making

**Stephen
Brookfield**
Reflection and
education
Adult learning

Julia Bamberger
Reflection and music

Jack Mezirow
Reflection and
education

Forester and Bolan
Reflection and planning

Peter Jarvis
Reflection and
nursing
Adult learning

Jan Fook
Reflection and social work

**Nick Gould and Imogen
Taylor**
Reflection and social work
Learning and professional
education

Chapter 4

Designing the Reflective Teaching Model

The previous two chapters have focused on the development of the notion of reflection from Dewey's move away from the dangers of 'habitual action', through Freire's conscientization, Habermas's emancipatory learning and Mezirow's perspective transformation, up to Schön's reflective practitioner. Having studied the reflective literature I became interested in designing a new teaching model that would allow health and social service professionals to work with service users in a in a more positive and equitable. This chapter outlines how I went about creating such a reflective teaching environment which drew on the work of the reflective theorists, but which also developed it further into a new, innovative reflective model. This chapter also begins to describe how, using an action research framework, this new teaching model was used with a group of health and social service professionals working in the area of intellectual disability.

Designing the Teaching Environment

As has been discussed in the last chapter, Schön highlighted a need for a 'practice environment' which is as near as possible to real-world practice. Such an environment would allow the reflective practitioner to fully develop his/her practice 'to experiment at low risk, vary the pace and focus of work and go back to do things over when it seems useful to do so' (Schön 1987: 170). Schön talks of the need to 'see' the learning process in the practicum and the need to see 'the practical work of modification, of changing, of reconstruction continued without end' (Dewey 1974: 7).

In order to create such a cycle of learning and change, I became interested in creating a practicum within which students could achieve increasing levels of critically reflective learning. Schön suggested that, by establishing such a reflective environment, the reflective teacher/researcher should be able to create a dialogue with students which would take the form of reciprocal reflection-in-action (1987: 163). Bamberger (1991: 46) proposed that the reflective researcher/teacher should view learning in the practicum as a series of reflective conversations, not only between teacher and students, but also between students and their 'materials', i.e. the individuals with whom they work. Such reflective conversations with materials require that students explore issues and problems as similar as possible to those they are likely to encounter in practice, with all their ambiguities and complexities (Reed and Procter 1993: 31-32).

I wanted to create a reflective environment that would enable students to engage in reflective learning in regard to their work with service users. In order to do so, I had to accomplish the following tasks:

- Create a practicum where students could explore and reflect upon the ambiguities and complexities of their on-going work with service users (in this case, parents of disabled children).
- Create opportunities where new approaches to clients, arising from such reflection, could be attempted and evaluated in a safe and supportive milieu.
- Create a learning environment that could evolve in response to the changing needs of the students.
- Create a learning environment where the participants' reflective development could be monitored and analysed in accordance with the criteria for a piece of action research.

Partialising the Learning Environment

A good reflective teaching environment should, by its nature, produce good reflective learning in students. However, I also wanted to be able to encourage, recognize and monitor the different phases of reflective learning that might occur within the practicum. As already demonstrated in Chapters 2 and 3, certain levels of commonality had been identified between phases of reflection as suggested by different writers and had constructed a grid that demonstrated such similarities. I wanted to use this grid to be a base upon which to design new, specific teaching techniques that would encourage reflective learning at specific stages in the reflective process. By identifying the stages in this way, I could then create a reflective teaching model which would maximize the natural learning which would be expected to occur as the students moved through the different phases of the reflective experience.

Although the reflective literature indicates specific phases in reflective learning, there appears to be some reluctance by theorists to try and identify the role of the reflective teacher in facilitating these different phases of reflective change. Schön, in particular, could be vague as to how the reflective teacher would precisely help the student to move from technical rationality to reflective practice. In his ideographic case studies (1983: 76-267; 1987: 41-255) Schön's reflective teachers work with students, primarily through the medium of performance, to achieve what he later described (1991: 5-9) as the critical 'reflective turn' in their practice. However, these journeys towards the reflective turn often appear as a seamless continuum from technical rationality to reflective practice – from Model I to Model II. I considered that it would be possible, by using a specific reflective teaching and learning model, to expose the students to a series of interlinked, reflective teaching stimuli which would be matched to specific stages of reflective learning. Thus, the practicum would have different reflective stages to enhance the students' accomplishment of the reflective turn. Such a reflective teaching and learning model would also allow me to monitor and analyse the reflective changes occurring at different times and in response to different learning stimuli. Therefore I developed five stages in this new teaching model, each of which would involve different and specifically designed learning stimuli appropriate to the learning needs and the reflective achievements identified as most likely to occur at each particular stage. These five new stages can be seen in Figure 4.1 and they are each discussed in depth in this chapter.

Model Rotation

Using the amalgam of the reflective learning stages (Figure 4.1) as a guide, I began to plan a new reflective teaching model that would address the specific learning needs at each of the stages. This model would try to help students to acknowledge, challenge and modify their perception of the service users with whom they worked and would be based on a reflective design that I called 'model rotation'. This idea takes the engineering notion of being able to rotate a model to increasing extents, in order to see aspects and perspectives hitherto unrevealed. This idea is akin to a computer-generated image being initially rotated by 180° to see a reverse dimension and then fully manoeuvred by a full 360° to achieve a number of different, three-dimensional viewpoints. By using this new concept of model rotation, I considered that students could be helped in a reflective practicum to take their conceptual models of clients and manipulate them in order to appreciate new standpoints and extra dimensions. By doing so they should begin to achieve Mezirow's (1991: 155-156) 'perspective transformation'. Stephen Brookfield (1995: 28) warns that, to some extent 'we are all prisoners trapped within the perceptual frameworks that determine how we view our experiences'. Brookfield (1995: 29) also talks of the need to 'stand outside ourselves' and the difficulty of achieving such a stance due to the human tendency to surround ourselves with people who share our own assumptions. This idea is closely linked to Argyris and Schön's notion of single-loop testing of ideas – assessing the validity of a theory-in-use by only seeking feedback from sources which confirm its efficacy. I thought that it would be unlikely that model rotation would occur spontaneously and that individuals, particularly those with more fixed assumptions, might need different teaching approaches through which they could be facilitated and encouraged to develop and evaluate new perspectives in their work. Taking the concepts of reflection, especially those developed by Argyris and Schön, I wanted to advance this idea of model manipulation and use it to meet the developing needs of a class of health and social care professionals.

Figure 4.1 Comparison of Stages of Reflective Learning III

Dewey	Habitual action	New data to inform situation	Intellectualization of problem Formulation of new hypothesis	Testing of new hypothesis	Reflection and evaluation of hypotheses
Mezirow	Unresolved dilemma based on habitual assumption	Trigger event	Perspective transformation	Emancipatory learning	Reflection on transformation
Habermas	Technical practice Objectified processes	Exposure to new ideologies	Reassessment of previous meanings	Emancipatory learning domain	Emancipatory learning with self-reflection
Brookfield	Habitual working practices	Trigger event	Discomfort, exploration of old working practices	Development of alternative perspectives	Integration of new approaches
Argyris and Schön	Tacit knowledge	Inconsistencies in practice exposed	Knowledge-on-action	Reflection-on-action and Reflection-in-action, double-loop testing	Critical reflection
	Relationship to phases in new reflective teaching and learning model				
New Reflective Model	Introduction to reflection	Exposure to new ideas	Simple model rotation	Full model rotation	Meta-reflection

Phases of the Reflective Teaching Model

I saw this new teaching and learning model as having five phases relating to the five identified stages of reflection. These phases would be developed in the manner of Kemmis and McTaggart's action research planner (1982), with each phase perceived as an action research cycle, having four distinctive levels of planning, action, observation and reflection. Thus, the application of the reflective teaching model would be regarded as a dynamic research process, leaving room for development and transformation within the research process as it progresses. By doing so, I planned to develop the reflective teaching and learning model into what Carr and Kemmis (1986: 10) describe as a critical theory of learning.

Phase I of the Reflective Model – Introductory Sessions

This phase of the research corresponds to what Mezirow called 'pre-reflection'. In this state learning can occur, but such learning would be expected to be characterized by typification – making interpretations based primarily on prior experience (1991: 16). These sessions would introduce the class to the idea of reflective learning which might, in itself, appear strange to professionals more used to connecting the university classroom with didactic teaching approaches. I also hoped that these sessions would allow me to gain an idea of the nature of the current interactions being achieved between the students and service users and to start to examine the overall attitudes in the class towards those with whom they worked. These sessions should also prepare students for their impending sessions with the two service users who would be acting as co-teachers with me.

Phase II of the Reflective Model – Exposure to New Ideas

The second phase of the teaching model would introduce service users into the classroom, in this case two mothers of disabled children. The purpose of including service users at this point was to expose the students to new data upon which they could begin to construct their own new perspectives of their clients. Dewey (1933: 100-101) saw this part of the process of reflective change as isolating the relevant data or subject matter, which would define the parameters within which reflection could occur. Such data would allow the practitioner to begin to move from habitual practice towards an intellectualization of that practice, leading to reflection on its efficacy. The act of having service users communicate their experience to the class also falls into Habermas's sphere of communicative action (1971: 309) which he saw as a precursor to emancipatory learning. Mezirow (1991: 65) saw communicative action as occurring whenever an individual with particular aims communicates with another person in order to arrive at an understanding about the meaning of a common experience. My previous work with parents of disabled children (1996: 78-80) had revealed their frustration about the difficulties they had encountered in their communications with professionals. Thus, giving parents this chance to communicate with professionals seemed to offer an opportunity to see if such interaction might initiate new understanding of service users by the professionals and be a precursor for reflective change.

I felt that hearing the personal accounts of individual service users would help move the students from what might be a removed typification of service users to a more individualized perspective. I also saw the service user-to-professional communication within this session as playing an important role in preparing professionals for the first levels of model rotation. Schön (1987: 35) suggested that, in order to begin to become reflective about their practice, practitioners must experience a 'surprise' which would lead them to re-think their knowing-in-action in a way that goes beyond available rules, facts, and theories. In other words, professionals may have to begin to doubt that the perceptions they hold are clear and unambiguous before they can be engaged in a process of reflection. I speculated that, by exposing students to the viewpoint of two service users, such doubt could be engendered which would provide an incentive for beginning to reflect-in-action.

Phase III of the Reflective Model – Simple Model Rotation

One of the unique aspects of this reflective teaching and learning model is the partialisation of the reflective process into simple model rotation and full model rotation. In simple model rotation the student is encouraged, through a specific methodology (called 'mirroring'), to begin 180° rotation of their perspective of the service user. This type of rotation challenges students to move from the expected typification of service users to an increased understanding of how they, as professionals, appear to the service users with whom they work. In simple terms, they are asked to 'see' themselves through the mirror of the service user's viewpoint and subsequently 're-see' the service user as a result of the experience. This notion of 'seeing' and then 're-seeing' is central to the concept of reflection. For Mezirow (1991: 119-123), perspective transformation (re-seeing) cannot occur before the individual recognizes and challenges the distorted assumptions of his existing perspectives (seeing). In my theory of simple model rotation the students would challenge any distorted assumptions inherent in a fundamental perspective of service users and this reflective exercise would then form the basis on which more complex perspective change could occur.

The time required for this aspect of the reflective teaching and learning model could not be determined at this point and would be dependent on the success and progress of the work on simple model rotation. An action research methodology allows for periods of observation, reflection and re-planning. Therefore I would consider the simple model rotation phase as a complete research cycle and would evaluate the progress made in the cycle before proceeding to the more complex full model rotation.

Phase IV – Full Model Rotation

I envisaged this stage of the reflective model as being very significant – it should reveal whether the previous stages had prepared the students to achieve critical reflection on their practice with service users. It should also embrace what Cranton (1994: 158) described as critical self-reflection, which is at the core of transformative learning. In terms of the stages of reflective learning, this is the phase of the research that should be characterized by the students' ability to reflect-on-action and reflect-in-action. The simple model rotation should have allowed students to see new aspects of both themselves and the service users but, arguably, these aspects might remain somewhat 'flat' and two-dimensional. The simple model rotation would also assist students to stand back and appreciate new aspects of the professional/parent interchange, rather like standing back from a painting in order to view it better. In full model rotation I wanted to create an environment where, through reflection, the students would be able to 'walk around' the interchange as if it were a piece of dynamic sculpture. In this phase of the teaching and learning model, the students should be able to 'walk around' not just their view of the service user the but also how they were interacting with clients, thus developing new, multi-dimensional perspectives on service users and on their interchange with them. Dewey described this type of reflection as the ability to 'turn a topic over in various aspects and in various lights so that nothing significant about it shall be overlooked, almost as one might turn a stone over to see what its hidden side is like or what is covered by it' (Dewey 1933: 57). Students would then use these new viewpoints to adjust and refine their practice as they began to better appreciate the complex nuances present in service users' reactions and behaviours and their own responses to these circumstances. Thus, an environment should be created which encouraged and facilitated the students to reflect-on-action and reflect-in-action.

The full model rotation phase draws on Argyris and Schön's (1974, 1996) work on action theory as discussed in Chapter 3. As already discussed, I had decided to simplify the authors' ideas to better fit into my evolving work with the class in a way which would be a logical extension of the simple model rotation exercise. I had chosen to use Argyris and Schön's method of case study presentations, because this approach had been used and comprehensively documented over a number of years (1974: 37-63; 1996: 123-149). I thought that their method of case study presentations would fit well at this point and would aid the students in fully rotating their perspectives of service users. As in Argyris and Schön's model of action theory, each student would be asked to produce a piece of work with service user/s that had been especially challenging (see Appendix B). The class would then attempt to analyse this work in relation to the concept of Model I and Model II behaviour. However, the analysis of the case studies would be undertaken using a newly designed Four-Question Case Audit that would involve the students more fully in the analysis than had been possible using Argyris and Schön's analytical techniques.

I also planned that the students would complete a written exercise during this phase of the research. I asked each student to choose a family with whom they were involved and to construct a brief plan for this family, outlining the most appropriate professional approach and support which they should receive in the immediate and longer term. Students were encouraged to complete this 'family plan' in consultation with the parents in order to help them continue the model rotation. The notion of the family plan was also to offer a written reflective exercise which would be complementary to the primarily verbal case study presentation, thus offering students different media through which to reflect on their practice. This recognition that different students would have strengths and weaknesses in disparate learning styles is supported by Brookfield's assertion that 'the principal of diversity should be engraved on every teacher's heart' (1990: 69).

I hoped that the work accomplished in the previous phase of the teaching and learning model in simple model rotation would prepare the students to undertake the more complex perspective changes inherent in full model rotation. The exposure to new ideas in phase two model and the subsequent third phase of simple model rotation allowed students to re-see some of their beliefs, attitudes and emotional reaction to service users. Mezirow (1990a: 2-3) called this transformation of meaning schemes. His research indicated that the transformation of meaning schemes was frequently the precursor to the transformation of meaning perspectives, involving critical self-reflection upon how meaning schemes constrain perceptions and understandings. Mezirow (1991: 167) suggested that, until perspective transformation occurs, students were not capable of acting upon such new understandings. If Mezirow's proposition was true, then this phase of the teaching and learning model should reveal whether the students were able to change their practice as a result of model rotation.

Like the previous phase of the teaching and learning model, the amount of time spent in this phase would depend on the progress made within it. I envisaged that, as the reflection expected of students would be more complex, this phase of the teaching and learning model would take longer than any of the others. Therefore I arranged for a relatively flexible number of hours to spend with the class in the latter weeks of the application of the model.

Phase V of the Reflective Model – Meta-Reflection

Many of the reflective theorists appear to see the end result of reflection as being a conscious change in practice brought about by a recognition and elimination of tacit, often distorted, attitudes and the adoption of newer, more pertinent perspectives of those with whom they work. Schön's goal for the reflective practitioner ends with reflective practice generated by reflection-in-action. As has been discussed in Chapter 2, all of Mezirow's seven levels of reflectivity (1981: 12-13) must be present in order to create reflection-in-action. For Mezirow, the transition from perspective transformation learning to emancipatory learning remains the highest point of what he described as 'sequential moment of meaning being clarified' (1991: 193).

There is, perhaps, a danger in seeing reflective practice or emancipatory learning as the irreversible end of a set of pre-determined procedural stages. Habermas (1974: 40-41) cautions that we are never in a position to know with absolute certainty that critical enlightenment has been effective. He warns that different forms of resistance, the inadequacy of intellectual understanding and, indeed, any claim of enlightened understanding may itself be a deeper and subtler form of self-deception (Bernstein 1985: 218-219). Based on my analysis of the literature and in order to avoid an over-simplification of the process, I decided that the fifth phase of the reflective teaching and learning model should be that of meta-reflection, or reflection upon reflection. This fifth phase would allow both me and the professional student to reflect upon and evaluate the development of the reflective teaching and learning model. The addition of such a phase also conformed to the principles of action research, which highlights the collaborative role of the research participant in both the implementation and the evaluation of the research. It is worth re-stating Argyris's (1985: 8-9) theory that action research involves effective re-education which depends on the freedom of the research participants to choose to become involved in the diagnosis of behaviour and the adoption of new kinds of action.

This final phase would mark the end of the my teaching contact with the class and would offer the students a chance to review the reflective teaching and learning model and to assess its effect on their current and future practice. This extra phase also gave me a platform from which to begin the final analysis of the success of the reflective teaching and learning model, where I could comment on and evaluate my own role as teacher and as researcher.

Finding a Research Perspective

The implementation of the teaching model could not happen in an arbitrary fashion and needs to be used within a clear research methodology. Bawden (1991: 21) notes that the choice of methods brought to an enquiry is related to the researcher's state of mind about the state of the world around him. As a trained social worker and a researcher into service users perspectives I had particular interest in the perception of many parents of disabled children that they were misunderstood and poorly treated by health and social service professionals (Redmond 1996, 1997, 2000, 2003). My experience had made me become increasingly aware of the lack of collaboration evident between many service users and professionals with whom they worked. For this reason it was important to choose a research method which would be collaborative by nature. Action research offers the participants a higher degree of self-determination and self-development capabilities which should continue after the research ends: 'This leads to fundamentally different relations

between researcher and those supplying the data and relies on a different
epistemology of inquiry' (Elden and Chisholm 1993: 27).

Action Research

Kurt Lewin (1946) coined the term 'action research' to describe a pioneering
approach to social research which combined the generation of theory to change the
social system by means of the researcher acting in or on that system.   Action
research was seen as a method of changing the system and generating critical
knowledge about it (Susman and Evered 1978: 586). Given that I would primarily
be acting in the role of teacher with a class of professionals, it was particularly
apposite that action research had become widely used in the area of teaching,
learning and educational theory. (Carr and Kemmis 1983). Carr and Kemmis
(1986: 179-213) coined the phrase 'educational action research' not only to
observe, record and describe work in the classroom, but also to widen the
perspective and make the investigation itself educational (McNiff 1988: 20).
Zuber-Skerritt (1992b: 52-54) recommends an action research approach to
facilitate constructing the meaning of practice for postgraduate university students.
Her research had demonstrated that such an approach results in metacognition or
'learning conversations' between student and teacher.

Circles and Spirals

Argyris (1985: 8) had noted that Lewin's action research model was characterized
by cycles of:

- planning
- action
- observation
- reflection.

The notion of circularity and spiralling has been further developed by other action
research theorists and the notion of planning, action and reflection is central to the
research process. Carr and Kemmis (1983) continued the development of the action
research spiral. They argued that a single-loop of planning, observing, acting and
reflecting was not sufficient and was not viable action research. They maintained
that the 'moment' of the action research cycle was a probe into the future. What
one learned in one cycle should be applied judiciously in further cycles, becoming
'an organized process of learning' (Carr and Kemmis 1983: 162).
    The notion of consecutive cycles of action research appealed to me as it
supported my wish to develop new directions in my work which could 'grow' out
of previous research phases. It also allowed for periods of reflection within the
research that seemed valuable both for me and the research. Having examined a
number of possible action research approaches, the one which seemed most

appropriate was Kemmis and McTaggart's procedural guide *The Action Research Planner* (1982). Kemmis and McTaggart's planner sets out clearly defined self-reflective spirals encompassing phases of planning, action, observation, reflection and re-planning. Although originally designed for research in the school system, Zuber-Skerritt (1992b: 16) believes that it is easily adapted to action research in higher education.

Practice/Theory Divide

I also wanted to attempt to find new solutions to the problems of the parent/professional divide. Elden and Chisholm (1993: 127) state that action research is change-oriented and attempts to use research processes that bring about change that has positive social value. Action research also deals with the practical concerns of people and is oriented towards creating a more desirable future for them (Susman and Everard 1978: 598). Action research offers the researcher the chance to bridge the gap between theory and practice. It provides an instrument through which theory and practice can be seen, not as two separate entities, but as two independent but complementary phases of the same change process. Winter (1996: 25) reminds us that theory and practice need each other and are indispensable parts of a unified change process: 'Together they present the strongest case for practitioner action research which represents both a powerful, vigorous and worthwhile form of practical professionalism and a powerful, vigorous and valid form of social enquiry'.

Images and Metaphors

My analysis of the reflective model also includes observation of imagery and metaphor, either recurring or created within the reflective teaching and learning model. Deshler (1990: 310-313) noted that, by reflecting on metaphors, individuals can be offered an opportunity to become more critical of possibly distorted perspectives. Deshler (1990: 312) also considers that the creation of new metaphors within the reflective teaching process contributes to the search for new meaning. Gould (1996b: 65-67) writes about the importance of recognizing imagery and metaphor, which he describes as word images, in a reflective learning environment. He notes that learners create images and metaphors as a way of making sense out of confusion and to construct their self-identity as professionals. I hypothesized that through the identification of both old and newly created metaphors and images, I would be able to gain insight into subtle perspective changes occurring throughout the teaching and learning model.

The Reflecting Researcher

An important aspect of using an action research framework for the implementation of the model was to allow for an analysis of my own contribution to the research process. Schön warns the reflective researcher that, in entering into a collaborative action research relationship with the participants 'she is personally on the line in a special way' (1991: 356). He cautions that the action researcher must strive to test her assessment of the situation, bringing to the surface, juxtaposing and discriminating among alternative accounts of that reality. A special section of the analysis of the whole research process in Chapter 8 is devoted to a reflection on my own perspective changes during the research and my own ability to reflect-in-action.

Summary

This chapter has set out the five phases of the reflective teaching model that was applied with a class of professional students. I will now begin, as Schön (1991: 345-347) puts it, to 'tell the story' of what occurred in my work with a groups of health and social service students over a period of six months. Schön's use of the word 'story' relates to that underlying story of the journey that both the research participant and the teacher/ researcher must make in order to achieve the 'reflective turn'. I had seen the need for openness, honesty and rigour in the application of the teaching and learning model and the analysis of its efficacy. I also noted Mezirow's (1991: 219-224) warning that reflective learning is about more than becoming aware of one's awareness. He has reminded the teacher/researcher that her job is to help learners look critically at their beliefs and behaviours, not only as they appear in the moment, but also in the context of how they work with people in the longer term. Mezirow has also cautioned that the reflective researcher must find a way to gain access to the meaning schemes and perspectives of the research participants. In subsequent chapters I will attempt to identify not only such meaning schemes and perspectives, but also chart the changes that evolved in them as the new teaching and learning model is put into practice.

Chapter 5

Phases I and II: Introduction and Exposure to New Ideas

Background to the Research

As part of my teaching at University College Dublin I was due to work for twenty-four classroom hours with a post-graduate class with whom I would explore new, reflective ways of interacting with service users. The class in question consisted of a group of health and social service professionals attending a part-time post-graduate course in Intellectual Disability Studies. At the start of the academic year I met these professional students and discussed the proposed research with them. The class consisted of twenty-three postgraduate students from a range of professions – nursing, social work, psychology, medicine, teaching, occupational therapy, childcare, management and administration. All except two students were in current practice in the area of intellectual disability and all had worked in the area at some point in their professional lives. The age range of the class extended from mid-twenties to early fifties, with a number of students having over twenty years of experience in the area of intellectual disability. I was able to negotiate that the time I worked with the class would always be their last session of the day, to help them put some distance between the earlier didactic teaching and the participatory nature of their work with me.

The progress of the work achieved in my sessions with these students were structured in accordance with Kemmis and McTaggart's 1981 *The Action Research Planner* and is presented in cycles of planning/action/reflection/re-planning. All the sessions with the class were simultaneously tape-recorded and video-recorded. The students attended university on a one-day per week basis, remaining in practice for the other four days. Their course ran for eight hours per day for twenty-four weeks over one academic year. Regular free research and library access periods were also scheduled and the students were provided with a total of one hundred and fifty contact teaching hours over the academic year. I used twenty-four of these contact teaching hours (16% of total contact teaching time) to work directly on my reflective teaching model.

During the course of the research, one student had to drop out of her studies temporarily due to illness and three other students had significant levels of absenteeism from classes. For this reason, nineteen students participated in the research. Of these, seventeen worked directly in services for those with learning

Reflection in Action

disability and their families; one worked with a group of frail, elderly patients; and one student had a private counselling practice. The students ranged in age from mid-twenties to late fifties. They came from a number of professional backgrounds, the largest of which was nursing, see Figure 5.1.

Figure 5.1 Professional Backgrounds of Research Participants

Profession	Number
Nursing	10 students
Psychology	3 students
Social Work	2 students
Medicine	2 students
Teaching	1 student
Occupational Therapy	1 student

Although the majority of students had come from a nursing background, not all of them were working in nursing posts – some were in working in administration, counselling and advisory services and family support work. All of the other professionals were working in posts based on their original professional training.

Not all professions require their practitioners to forge social and emotional relationships with their clients. A common link between the six professions represented in this research is that they all fit Goode's (1969: 297-304) description of 'person professions'. Goode defined 'person professionals' as those who, by the nature of their work, require clients to disclose intimacies to them, a fact that renders the client more vulnerable within the client/professional relationship. Ellis (1992: 69-70) described these professionals as 'interpersonal', their primary method of work being face-to-face interaction with clients.

All but two of the students were attached to a variety of different agencies providing services to those with learning disability and their families. Some students were working in agencies that were institutional in nature, offering residential care; others worked in settings that provided day, respite and outreach services for younger children and their parents. The agency settings of the students varied from rural settings with small numbers of clients, to large urban agencies catering for hundreds of individuals with disability and their families. The students came from all over the country and some travelled over 200 miles to attend the course each week. To protect the anonymity of the participants, reference will only be made to the professional background of each of the students.

Phase I of the Reflective Teaching Model – Introductory Session

Kemmis and McTaggart's action research planner (1982: 15-16) cautions the researcher to be specific in the planning involved in each stage of the research. This involves providing a description of the general idea that has lead to the first action step, those involved in the action and what was to be attempted. Much of the rationale for these sessions and the general planning behind them has already been discussed. This section will describe the specific planning which went into this phase of the research.

Planning

Summary of the Purposes of Phase I

- To allow the researcher and students to meet and to offer the students a general outline of their sessions together.
- To acquaint the students with the concept of adult learning in general and to give them a brief introduction to the theory of reflection.
- To gain an overall picture of the types of relationships these students have with the parents with whom they work.
- To discover the nature of the perspectives these students have about the parents.
- To monitor if these perspectives had any similarities towards those categories put together by me in my preliminary review of the literature.

Action

At the beginning of the first session I provided the class with some information about the work to be done together, with dates and times of classes. During the first hour of this session I asked the students for permission to video and audiotape the classes and the confidential aspects of the research were explained to them.

I also used some of this session to do work with the class on the nature of adult learning. The students were offered the opportunity to become involved in some group exercises to enable them to recognize the learning styles that suited them best. The class also completed an eco-map (see Appendix A). This involves the students exploring the structure of their employing agency in a visual/artistic manner – this exercise was designed by me to introduce the students to a reflective 'hands-on' style of working in the classroom. Because the exercise was also drawn and written it provided an exercise that all students could participate in, rather than introducing an exercise that favoured the more vocal students in the class.

The eco-map also allows students to produce a visual representation of the complex connections in their workplace. Used in family work it offers opportunities for family members to see the nature of the relationships between different elements of their life system which may be either supportive, stressful, encouraging or openly hostile (Hartman and Laird 1983). I used organizational eco-maps as a way of getting the practitioners to visualize the complex connections within their employing organization, to map the different sub-systems that exist within it and to note the nature of their own relationship with each element in the system. Importantly I asked the students to note in the eco-map where they felt that service users were situated in the agency hierarchies and how powerful they seemed to be in terms of decision making. The organizational sub-systems and the nature and quality of their inter-relationships between them (such as strong, supportive, hostile etc) were portrayed in the eco-map by the traditional symbols used in family eco-maps and genograms (see Hartman and Laird 1983, McGoldrick and Gerson 1985).

Observation

Reaction to the Reflective Environment

Although much of the reflective literature speaks about creating a reflective teaching environment, there seems to be little or no mention of how such an environment may appear unusual to students, especially those who expect a more traditional, didactic teaching milieu. There was an initial degree of surprise noted from some of the students that I would not be using a traditional lecturing approach. I was glad that I had planned time within Session One to discuss this aspect of my work and to reassure students that, unlike other modules on the Diploma course, there would be no exam in my work with them. In spite of this, three students subsequently asked if they would need to take notes during the class and one of the nurses reacted to the eco-map exercise by saying: '*this is like being back in kindergarten, I can't draw.*' Although I had anticipated that the reflective teaching environment would be different to what the students had expected on a university-based course, I had underestimated just how strange it would appear to some of the students. This reaction reinforces Schön's argument about the university's over-emphasis on the didactic teaching of scientific-based theory and how, as Cohen (1985: 180) notes, practice-based issues may be considered inferior and given sparse attention in an academic environment. Therefore, a good deal of the early part of the first two sessions was spent in reassuring and encouraging students that this would be a different, but not inferior, type of learning experience to a theory-based class. By the latter half of the first session, the students seemed more relaxed and the quality of discussion recorded in the last ninety minutes of the session yielded most of the useful data.

Categorization of Service Users

Having spent a good deal of time working with the students to help them feel comfortable in the class, I introduced some discussion about their perceptions of the service users with whom they worked. A review of the class transcripts revealed that the students' references to parents were not related to specific parents, rather to parents as a general group. When analysed, the students' references to parents during this session fell into three distinct areas:

- Parents who are misunderstood and badly treated by the system.
- Parents who are difficult to work with.
- Parents who are a barrier to helping the individual with learning disability.

Parents who are Misunderstood or Badly Treated This first category represented approximately 80% of all the references to parents in this first phase of the research. Some of the comments recorded related to parents whom the students felt had been poorly treated by other professionals and by the systems that provided services for those with learning disability and their families:

Nurse: There is not enough made available for them, they need a lot of help and individually you can only offer so much.

Social Worker: They are ignored a lot of the time not listened to, then they get angry with frustration.

Doctor: They have to take what's there, rather than what they really need in terms of services, then the service providers are annoyed that they aren't more satisfied with what's being offered.

Nurse: Parents often feel they are afraid to complain, that they'll be seen as a 'baddie'. That they will be seen as disruptive, like who would they be to voice criticism? They then give that reinforcement to us by saying that we're all-knowing, you know, we are the experts, you know best.

Nurse: They are required to be grateful a lot of the time, not to make trouble, the services really like thankful parents.

In many incidences, the students talked of parents who were not consulted by professionals and who, in consequence, were frequently offered either inadequate or inappropriate services. The students themselves did not seem to imply that parents were asked to be grateful for the services they received, but they implied that other professionals expected this of parents. Indeed, all except one of the recorded comments about parents referred to the insensitive behaviour of other professionals towards parents. The only reference that implies any personal involvement in the poor treatment of service users came from a psychologist:

> Psychologist: We need a wake-up call so that professionals can really look at how they are behaving, and I include my own profession [psychology] and social work as well. We're a long way off getting it right with parents.

The fact that the psychologist's remark was unique in including any form of personal causation for parental behaviour indicates that the students tended, in this and subsequent categories, to distance themselves from parents and to discuss them in terms of generalities. Mezirow (1991: 16) called this 'typification' which he saw as a limited method of making interpretations and construing meaning in problematic situations. He placed it within the sphere of unreflective and habitual practice. Certainly although many of the students appeared sympathetic to service users who were treated dismissively, none of the students, except one of the psychologists, indicated that they might have any role in changing the situation.

Parents Who Are Difficult to Work With   In this second category, which accounted for over one-third of the student responses, quite a negative typification of parents was demonstrated. However, some students qualified their remarks by connecting such negative parental behaviour to frustration and anger resulting from poor service provision and neglect:

> Nurse: I don't like to say it, but some of them can be very pushy. No matter what you do, it won't be right.

> Nurse: They are demanding. They need a lot and expect us to provide it.

> Social Worker: Sometimes you try very hard to get something for them, it takes a lot of effort, then they say, 'is that all?'. You never seem to get it right sometimes. After a while you sometime don't feel like trying any more.

> Nurse: We can only offer what we have, but it never seems enough.

Again, these remarks indicate a view of parents which has little connection with the actions of the individual professional. Indeed, these professionals seemed to consider that much of what they did for parents was unappreciated. This generalization is also relevant as it contains an underlying suggestion that parents who are difficult and ungrateful may be the architects of their own misery. Notice the comments *'no matter what you do it won't be right'* and another *'after a while you don't feel like trying any more'*. These comments suggested that by being difficult service users ostracise themselves from the help which professionals can give, thereby causing themselves more problems. More worryingly, they also imply that since service users may blame professionals for the shortcomings of others, it may be fruitless for professionals to try to work co-operatively with them at all. Again, as in the first category, this perception of service users does not indicate the need for any change on behalf of the professional. Faults are seen to be in the paucity of service provision on one hand and the unreasonable response to this by parents on the other and the professionals appeared to see themselves as unwitting victims caught between the two.

Obstructive Parents The third category of parents mentioned (approximately 20% of responses) also contained a perception of parents as unreasonable – as overprotective and obstructive against the reasonable wishes of the professional. Here the students referred to parents who were unwilling or obstructive towards professionals becoming engaged in work that would increase the independence of their adult children.

Nurse   But where do you draw the line when the person is an adult? How much do you allow the parent to control that person's adult life?

Nurse: They get stuck in seeing their adult child as helpless and won't consider change. Sometimes it just seems like selfishness.

Occupational Therapist: Through overprotection they can rob their adult children of a decent life. That doesn't seem fair to either that person or the staff who work with him or her.'

This perception of service users as a barrier to progress contains the powerful argument that parents' obstructive behaviour not only frustrates the professionals, but has much more serious consequences for the well-being of the adult with disability on whose behalf the professional is interceding. None of the references in this third category made any mention as to why parents might have valid reasons for not agreeing to changes in their adult child's life. The overall impression gained from the references was that, by championing the rights of the young adult, professionals were engaged in a virtuous activity. By disagreeing with them, parents were either overprotective or unsympathetic to the needs of their child. Again the underlying suggestion appears to be that the only change which could bring about improvement would be change by the parents.

'Dealing' with Parents

Another factor emerging from this introductory session was the adherence of many of the students to their professional boundaries. The first category of responses noted in this regard related to how some of the students saw their work with parents as being constrained by their profession:

> Nurse: As a nurse I wouldn't have that much to do with parents, maybe talk to them on the phone or when they call to the unit.

> Nurse: In our agency it's mostly the social worker who deals with the parents, we only meet them now and then, then it's usually just to chat about day to day stuff, how their son is getting on, that sort of thing.

These comments seem to indicate a belief that service users need to be 'dealt with' by a specific professional. They also imply that only some professionals have the required skills to 'deal with' parents. This concurs with Schön's idea (1987: 32-36) that, from a technically rational perspective, a community of professionals may share a socially and institutionally structured context. Within such a context, certain professions may be seen as having specialized and often-unique skills for operating within particular situations. The nature of technically rational thinking also implies that, unless one is trained within such a profession, one would not have the required technical skills to address certain issues. Schön (1987: 34) refers to this as 'thinking like a --------- ', implying that non-reflective professionals can only think and behave within the confines of a specific professional persona. What some of the students (all of them nurses) seem to imply in the above quotes is that, unlike social workers, they do not have the skills to deal with parents in a professional manner.

As the session progressed the issue of professional divides re-occurred. Arising from the idea that only certain professions could 'deal' with parents, a number of students discussed what they saw as the poor treatment many parents received from these other professionals:

> Psychologist: Some of the attitudes towards parents can be so dismissive. Only last week I saw a woman who has spent twenty years taking care of her son and this particular professional put down, because she had made a mistake with his medication, he put down *'Mother as usual has messed things up again'*. This was written down on an official file.

> Social Worker: I think those attitudes come mostly from doctors, they can be so dismissive of what parents are trying to do.

An argument developed between three nurses, a psychologist and a doctor in the class. The main thrust of the argument was how nurses in particular have to 'pick up the pieces' after parents have been dealt with by insensitive doctors.

Nurse: It's like they don't think about what they are telling parents and they don't give them a chance to ask questions. Then we [nurses] we have to spend time with them afterwards, trying to deal with their upset.

Psychologist: How much help do you think it is if somebody tells you your child is going to be a vegetable? Parents get told stupid things like that, then they find out it's not true.

Doctor: Who would be told that?

Nurse: A lot of people are told that sort of stuff by doctors. They put themselves forwards as experts and the parents are given the message 'I know best, don't question what I tell you'.

Doctor: That's rubbish.

Nurse: No it's not. You'd be surprised how many parents get told stupid things by doctors. It's like they presume they know better than parents do, like they can never know as much as the mighty doctor.

The above conversation indicates that a number of the students criticize a technically rational 'expert' stance towards parents, but only recognize it in other professions. As well as these students mentioned above, six other students used words such as 'dismissive', 'judgemental' and 'insensitive' about their experiences of doctors working with parents.

Images and Metaphors

Social Worker: Certainly a lot of parents have been treated really badly in the past, especially the older ones. But we were not responsible for that yet we often get caught in the middle.

This comment exemplifies the most common image emerging from this session – the professional caught in the middle between the 'bad' service and its victim, the complaining parent. Other students had used the terms 'caught' or 'stuck' in the middle to describe the dilemma. In their eco-maps, another five students prepared a graphical representation of their agency that placed themselves between the service provider and the parents, all indicated that the relationship in this position was antagonistic or hostile. This imagery can also be extended to include some of the professional boundary-keeping, discussed above. Again in the eco-maps, four of the students placed themselves as being entangled in antagonistic or hostile relationships between doctors and parents. This image of being an innocent observer caught between two hostile factions may further remove the professional from the need to effect change in his or her own practice. It was noted that no student talked of testing the validity of the image by engaging with individual parents to see how they perceived the situation, nor did any student suggest that they could advocate with others on behalf of parents.

Reflection and Re-planning

During this introductory session I attempted to introduce the students to the idea of working in a reflective practicum and to begin the implementation of my new reflective teaching and learning model. One of my starting hypotheses – that the professionals may lack a multi-dimensional perspective on the service users that they encounter – seems borne out by the manner in which these students described parents. The students' perspective on parents in this session appeared to be relatively generalized, with parents bracketed into a number of distinct categories that lack complexity or definition. Another initial finding was that students appeared constrained by their professional role in their interactions with parents, seeing specific professions as those which 'deal' with families.

This session helped me to focus on the structure and purpose of the next phase of the teaching and learning model – the introduction of two parents of disabled children into the class who would conduct the next session of teaching/research with me. In order to continue the move away from a technically rational, didactic classroom approach, I structured the parents' session in order to maximize the participative nature of the interaction. In the three weeks between the first and second session I asked the students to begin preliminary work on a written family plan, which they would complete by the end of the course. This exercise was designed again as a reflective device, but also one which would help the students begin to move from the generalized categorization of parents to a more individualized, objective perspective. I designed this exercise to help the students to begin to reflect on how they appreciated the parental viewpoint. In this way I sought to create a medium through which the students could begin to experience Mezirow's   (1991: 6) reflective learning which involves assessment or reassessment of assumptions, leading to a transformation of ways of interpreting experience.

Phase II of the Reflective Teaching and Learning Model – Exposure to New Ideas

Planning

Summary of the Purposes of Phase II

- To allow two service users to talk to the class about their experiences and to give the students the opportunity to discuss with them their own current work with parents. The fact that these parents would be perceived as teachers was intended to be an important factor in lending credibility to their viewpoints. It would also allow the class to see the two parents as distinct individuals rather than as part of an amorphous group to whom generalities could apply.
- To allow the class to hear first-hand testimony from parents with whom they have no work relationship, which would help introduce a more objective perspective on parental concerns.

Action and Observation

Following consultation with the two parents involved, this session was structured so that each parent had time to talk about her experiences of being a mother of a disabled child with the class. Suzanne is the mother of Tim, aged eight at the time of the session, who has Down's Syndrome and who was then attending a local integrated school. Suzanne was working full-time in the home at the time and had considerable involvement in developing workable systems of integrated education in Ireland. Suzanne has been a member of a group of parents involved in a national association of parents of disabled children who meet with students in areas as medicine, speech therapy and nursing to talk about the experience of being a parent of a child with intellectual disability.

Tess's son Roger (aged twenty-eight at the time of this session) has a profound level of intellectual disability. Roger is deaf and has no speech, his only voluntary movement is in one arm and he uses a wheelchair. At the time of the session Roger was working two days a week in a local library where his employment was supported by a job coach. Tess had worked at management level in an agency for those with intellectual disability and she had experience of both hiring and training professionals and of working with other parents and families.

I had heard both these woman speak at different conferences within the previous year and had approached them about the possibility of working with me. Before the class, the women discussed with me how they would like to structure their four-hour session. The first part of the session was to consist of both Suzanne and Tess talking generally about their experiences with professionals in the past. The mothers then wanted to use the second half of the session to develop areas introduced earlier with the students. Both the mothers and I were happy to leave the latter half of the session relatively unstructured in order to be open to accommodate any developments between parents and students that might occur.

My role in this session was that of group facilitator. I would help the mothers co-ordinate the session and my intention was to engage only in minimal intervention in the interaction between parents and students. However, I also wished to maintain the reflective ethos started in the previous session, by discussing matters with the parents and with the class. This would include my own modelling of the use of critical questioning in a limited manner during the session, encouraging its use amongst the students. Questioning is considered critical when it prompts responses which require thought and consideration and when it fosters reflection rather than eliciting information. Stephen Brookfield (1987: 92) calls critical questioning 'one of the most effective means through which assumptions can be externalized'.

Observation

Early Experiences

Both parents began by talking to the class about their early experiences. Tess's story was, perhaps, initially more striking than Suzanne's, in that she had begun her long relationship with professionals twenty years earlier and her son's disability has involved far more serious medical complications. As a mother of other children, she had serious concerns about her then infant son's health – her earliest encounters with the medical profession marked the beginning of a the long battle of to persuade someone that something was very wrong with him.

> Tess: I presented my darling to the doctor again and he looked at me and he squinted his eyes up and he said *'you are the fussiest mother I've ever come across in my life'*. A few days later I still was really worried about Roger and I went in again and he said *'not you again'*.

Tess's experience of not having her intuition and insights into her son's health acknowledged by is clearly recorded in the literature (Dale 1996, Read 2000). Parents of disabled children report that professionals assert the supremacy of their knowledge with the attendant attitude that parents should be grateful to be recipients of such superior wisdom. In Schön's (1983: 30-32) terms, the technically rational professional has no need of other insights into his epistemology of practice – everything he requires lies within his existing empirical scientific knowledge base. Such a stance also negates any motivation to view matters from a parental perspective as evidenced from another doctor's consoling words to Tess on her deaf and severely disabled baby.

Tess: And I was pleading for support in preparing for our son's dark silent life – how we could help him, get ready for him coming home, and to help him. And I didn't expect that man to take me by the hand. All I wanted was for him to point me in a direction – to say: *'you know who you need to talk to?'* That's all I needed. But I didn't get it. What I got was a fairly paternalistic pat, a little pat on the shoulder, and he said to me: *'Don't worry too much, my dear, because the likelihood of him living any longer than six months is remote. And then your worries will be over'*.

The diagnosis of Suzanne's son's Down's Syndrome was less traumatic, but she confirmed the sense of inadequacy many parents experience at the realization that having a child with disability implies that, as a family, they may now be perceived as being qualitatively different and in need of professional expertise.

Suzanne: When Tim came along, all our experience as parents counted for nothing. When we were leaving the hospital with him we were given a piece of paper with the phone number of our local learning disability agency written on it. Can you begin to imagine how resentful that piece of paper made me feel? Here was I bringing my beautiful baby – my third baby – home from hospital and his Dad and his brothers and I weren't going to be enough for him. We weren't going to be able to embark on this adventure on our own and would have to bring assorted strangers along for the ride.

The sense of being pathologised into a 'handicapped family' runs through Suzanne's account, particularly her difficulty in entering the new, often labyrinthine, world of the multi-disciplinary professional team. When it came to the time for her son to attend school, she found that he could not automatically enter his local school, as his brothers had done. Instead, a psychologist had to meet the family, then meet with the school staff to 'negotiate' a place in the school for him.

Suzanne: We were not allowed to talk to the school about his suitability, this was the job of a professional, even though we knew the school and we knew Tim's abilities, this was not enough. Another thing that we found extremely difficult was that we now had a social worker. We had assumed that only people who were in some sort of difficulty with which they couldn't cope had a social worker and we didn't feel ourselves to be in that category. I found the feeling that I was being analysed and assessed very disconcerting. We are incensed beyond imaging to have the birth of our much-loved child described as a 'family tragedy'... or to be asked *'have you come to terms with it yet?'*

Suzanne's was describing her frustration at the professional assumption that feelings of grief and loss must inevitably follow the birth of a child with disability. This is a good example of the Model II professional assumption that families are operating in a grief and bereavement scenario, even when they display no overt indications that this is the case.

Images and Metaphors – Women in Combat

A characteristic of both women's accounts to the class was the recurring theme of their necessity to combat the health and social service systems in which they found themselves. The women repeatedly referred to themselves as fighters and stressed their continuing need to fight both for themselves and for their children. In many of the situations which they described to the class, this fighting seemed to represent a metaphor for their resistance to professionalism and bureaucracy – their refusal to become part of a professional schema which failed to acknowledge them and their expertise about their child. Gould (1996: 65) sees the use of metaphor as a reflexive process by which humans actively categorize experience, where their own subjectivity is constructed through images and metaphors that are current in their 'forms of life'. In the cases of Tess and Suzanne, they articulated their need to fight against professional structures that could not or would not recognize the individual needs of their child. They also seem to have had to combat systems, which put them in the position of untutored recipients grateful for services over which they have no control. Both women expressed surprise that they took up the mantle of the fighter, as it seemed out of character for them. Tess described herself as a basically very shy person:

> Tess: But I realized that shy wasn't going to help my son – that I was going to have to turn into a semi-fishwife, because I decided I was going to fight and I'd fight the devil himself. He's your child and who else is going to know him so well and fight for his human rights?

> Suzanne: Make no mistake, my life is a battle now. There are professionals, civil servants and politicians who groan when they hear my voice on the phone or see my signature on a letter. The biggest talent I have developed since Tim's birth is to make a nuisance of myself, which is a poor indictment of our society and its attitude to people with disability.

Since the mothers had described how they had to 'learn' to fight, the action being contrary to their usual demeanour, it was necessary to see what effect this had had on them. This was an opportunity for me to model a critical question for the students:

> Researcher: But is there a personal cost, a cost to you of having to be such fighters?

> Tess: Yes, you have to keep chipping away at the professional monolith – to get the needs of the individual person and family recognized. Just sometimes it

feels like trying to move a mountain with a teaspoon – it can be done, but it takes such a long time.

Suzanne: You know, I resent the time it takes and the time it causes me to spend away from Tim and my other children. So, you're right, we have to keep chipping away, but I can't get over my resentment that it should be necessary.

Tess: To answer your question, it can get really hard sometimes to find the energy to fight. A fire can only burn brightly for a limited time, and it can be refuelled then, and sometimes the simplest thing can refuel your fire. Sometimes it's an injustice, not even to your own child but to somebody else, and you say that's a raw bloody deal, and they're not getting away with that! And you go at it – you fight again.

Working with the Class

Following the individual accounts given by Tess and Suzanne, the students then began to discuss some of the issues raised by the two mothers. I started the second part of the session by asking the women what qualities they looked for in good professionals. The purpose of this line of enquiry was to help the class to see how parents may view professionals, a preparation for forthcoming reflective work.

Tess: What do I look for in a good professional? Respect for the individual. In any profession, you've got to respect that each individual brings with them gifts, and that it's up to us to identify those gifts and offer them the opportunity to present those gifts. Respect for the individual, that is the core driving force that, if you respect a person, you can't do wrong by them.

Suzanne: Someone who will work with you, that is willing to aim high. I'd always prefer a person to approach me with an optimistic mindset, *'he's a great little fellow, let's you and I work together on this'*. I've had an occasional speech therapist, or whatever, over the years that will say, *'we'll go for it, we're going to teach him this, let's set ourselves these aims'*. This fires me up and I get so pleased. And if we don't make it, so what, we tried together.

A class member asked the parents what kind of professionals they felt had been most helpful to them in the past. The parents' responses indicated their desire for real equality in the parent/professional relationship:

Tess: Somebody who is honest with you. We're no fools and we don't like to be patronized. We shouldn't be treated like we have a learning disability as well.

Suzanne: My current social worker is brilliant, she feels more like a friend.

Researcher: What is it about her, what characterizes the way she works with you,
that you find helpful?

Suzanne: This is going to sound strange, but the girl who is my current social
worker seems to have had some personal sadness in her life. It's not like we've
discussed it, but I get the sense she has a personal handle on things that don't go the
way you want them to, things going wrong in your life. And I feel like I meet her
more on equal terms. She doesn't tell me what to do, or what I should or shouldn't
be feeling – she listens to me. She doesn't claim to have all the answers, we can
meet more or less on equal terms, that's great.

Suzanne had described many of the characteristics inherent in a Model II,
reflective practitioner – one who is not the only one in the situation with relevant
and important knowledge (Schön 1983: 300). Suzanne's perception of the
professional's 'personal sorrow' seemed to allow her to see the social worker as
more human, as less likely to expect perfection in others when there may be
imperfection in her own life. For Suzanne, this appears to have helped to
'equalize' the relationship. It would also seem that the social worker was adopting
a reflective approach when, in Schön's terms (1983: 300-302) she actively sought
out connections with Suzanne's thoughts and feeling – *'she listens to me'*.
Suzanne also noted that the professional's work was dependent on information and
actions that only Suzanne can undertake: *'she doesn't tell me what to do'*.

Equality

It is important to note that both mothers consistently mentioned the need for
equality in their relationship with professionals. Tess talked of respect for the
individual and the need to value and not patronize parental contributions. Suzanne
valued the optimistic professional who is willing to work with her, towards a
mutually agreed goal. The notion of equality lies behind the reflective practitioner
who must foster equality in order to hear and act upon responses gathered from the
client. Equality is also an integral part of Model II behaviour. One of the main
social virtues of Model II practice is that because of its inherent commitment to
equality, it increases the clients' capabilities to confront their own ideas and to
respect other people's capacity for self-reflection (Argyris and Schön 1996: 120).

Characteristics of Questions

The characteristics of the questions posed by the students to the parents were
another indication of the level of reflection they are applying to their practice.
Some questions contained Model I attributes, while other students asked critical
questions with Model II qualities. This can be seen by comparing the difference
between the question asked by two of the students. In response to Suzanne talking
of her desire to keep Tim in mainstream education, one of the nurses asked:

Nurse: About the future. How do you think Tim will be able to match up with your expectations of him, now it probably hasn't happened yet, but when his local peer group start to move away from him in the teenage years?'

This question contains a number of Model I characteristics. The student states what appears to be a technically rational fact – disabled teenagers get left behind by their intellectually-able peers. She says to Suzanne '*when Tim's peer group start to move away*', a statement that seems not to acknowledge that there might be something unique in Tim's situation which could circumvent such an outcome. By holding this theory, which implies an unconvertible truth held by a professional, there is also a clear suggestion that Suzanne's expectations of Tim might be naive, over-optimistic, or both. This supports a perception of parents as not being capable of having an objective view of their child's disability – the problem already referred to by Suzanne when she and her husband could not negotiate Tim's entry into his local school, but had to allow professionals to decide the issue. Suzanne answered the question well:

Suzanne: Yes, this is a huge difficulty. But he also belongs to a gymnastic club which is a mixed group and he belongs to a music class which is only for children with Down's Syndrome. So, I'm trying to make friends for him across the spectrum, but I must say that the whole idea of secondary education is a huge anxiety. I just – I have fought so many battles to have him accepted in primary school, and to get a resource teacher and all the rest of it. I'm just kind of now thinking about girding my loins for the next one.

Suzanne demonstrated that she had not accepted Tim's rejection by his intellectually-able friends as a given, but she had also taken steps to maximize his circle of friends, both disabled and non-disabled. Again, the fighting metaphor emerged, here the fighting was not to overcome the problems of making friends, but fighting against a system which implies that Tim will not 'fit' into an integrated educational system. Suzanne's answer also gave a new twist to the notion of accepting a child with disability. Here it was not, as is so often suggested, the parent who cannot accept the child, but the 'normal' social and professional systems that could not accept Tim's special needs.

In a different vein, another student asked a question which fulfils Brookfield's (1987: 92) definition of a critical question, one which demonstrates that the questioner is capable of externalizing and examining tacit assumptions.

Doctor: There is so much talk about partnership with parents, but really precious little seems to work out. What do you think professionals need to do to make it really happen?

This question had, in Suzanne's terms, a lot more equality. The student was stating that a widely articulated theory – partnership – might not exist in practice, thus challenging a tacit assumption. Her recognition of this lack of congruence between assumption and reality is an important reflective characteristic of Model II behaviour. The student was also willing to ask the parents how *they* think professionals can change, thus acknowledging that their input is important for professionals to learn how to change their practice. Tess's answer demonstrates her ability to be both objective and subjective about the issue.

> Tess: Successful collaboration is dependent on two things. One of the things is that there be collaborative advantage, meaning that each side in the collaboration has something to gain from this collaboration. There also has to be an agreed objective, and certainly, most professionals that I have found have the exact same objective as parents which is to deliver the best possible service to the person with disability. Parents don't pretend to know about learning disability in general, we only know about the one that we've got ourselves. And you've majored in that child, I can tell you. You have a master's degree in that child. Professionals ask me: *'How do you know he has a headache?'* Because I do know, because he squinges over one eye, his eyebrow goes up and it squinges and when I put my hand on it, he smiles as if he's saying *'That's it, Mother'*.

As well as illustrating that a good Model II question is likely to elicit a good answer, Tess, in describing how she diagnoses Roger's headache, is also demonstrating a perfect example of tacit knowing (Polanyi 1967: 9-10). She 'knows' when her son has a headache; Roger confirms, wordlessly that she is right, but it is difficult to make Tess's diagnostic skill explicit. This highlights what may be an important issue in the professional/service user relationship, the fact that much service user expertise is, by its nature, individual and primarily tacit in nature. Thus professionals, who tend to look for general and explicit theories, may find it hard to translate this expertise into a recognizable professional 'language'. In fact Tess even used a word, 'squinge', which she had invented, to describe the critical movement Roger makes with his eyebrow. It seems that her knowledge of Roger is so unique that she has had to create a special word to describe it. The difficulty is finding a place for such a unique word in a professional vocabulary that has problems incorporating 'lay-person' language, even when it exists in a dictionary.

The class ended with a general discussion between the students and parents. Towards the close of the session Tess, unprompted, adopted a reflective position, 'seeing' how parents may look from a professional perspective, as she discussed the balance between rights and responsibilities for parents becoming involved in more equitable relationships with professionals.

> Tess: I think that we parents too hold our little bit of power. It's innate in human nature not to give it away, and to expect professional people just to give their power away willy-nilly is kind of asking too much. Another thing that parents forget a little bit, I think, is that in partnership there's duties expected, it

comes with responsibilities. Occasionally, even when professionals are really working towards improving services, you get the odd parent who can be very much into being a victim and sort of dependent, *'poor me, no one's doing anything for me'*. That attitude, when it's not justified, can be destructive as a pushy professional. It has to be changed into a real joint effort to work together. Where families are involved in the development of services from a very young age, with their child and the service providers, the outcomes are much more positive.

What Tess had done here is central to reflective learning. She developed the general concept of power brokerage within the professional/service user relationship and also reflected on tacit parental behaviour within such a power struggle. By doing so she gave the class another way to view the relationship and did so while using Model II characteristics of minimal defensiveness about potentially difficult parental behaviour.

Reflection and Re-planning

The class was very engrossed during the session, they participated fully and interacted positively with the parents. This was revealed by the attention they paid to the parents as captured on video, and by the fact that all students spoke at least once during the session. This was also borne out by their later written evaluation of the session, in which it received more positive comments from the students than any other individual session. All the students rated the teaching content 'interesting' or 'very interesting' and the session's relevance for their practice was rated as 'relevant' or 'very relevant'. Ten of the nineteen students added positive comments about the session such as *'thought provoking'*, *'made you think'*, *'made me look at parents differently'* and *'illuminating'*. The student evaluations for the session showed other comments such as:

Nurse: This session made a huge impact on me. To see something through the eyes of a parents makes your job and what you decide to do every day seem very important.

Teacher: This approach to understanding the way parents feel was very appropriate and was really effective.

Many of the parents' experiences shared during the session showed a relationship between professional and service user that had inherent difficulties. Tess's experiences, perhaps because they related to an earlier time, had contained more marked examples of being dismissed by professionals who seem to fit the characteristics of Argyris and Schön's Model I practitioner. Both mothers had experience of being placed into the role of grateful or unknowing parents who needed the skills of professionals to help cope with their child. Both mothers talked of being pathologised, as being seen as a member of a family who, since they have a child with disability, are now fundamentally different and less able to function. Their repeated use of the 'battle' metaphor reinforced how both women feel the need to rail against such categorization, although they both admit to a personal cost of their continuing fight.

Both mothers explored aspects of their lives with considerable candour. Each aspect of the women's ability to reflect on their situation was very well developed with Tess, in particular, able to alternate between the parent and professional viewpoints. Suzanne identified unexpected reasons for her favourable response to her social worker, especially when she identified the social worker's own personal sorrow as a factor which equalized the relationship between them. It was this ability to manoeuvre perspectives on events that I tried to develop with the class in the forthcoming sessions.

During this second phase of the reflective teaching and learning model, I was able to introduce some aspect of critical questioning and was able to continue the reflective practicum begun in the previous session. There was a two-week gap before phase three of the reflective teaching and learning model. During this time the students were asked by me to meet with the family with whom they were preparing the family plan. I designed this exercise to assist those students who did not meet parents on a regular basis to begin to develop a more objective view of an individual family and their concerns. Such objectivity would become central to the next phase of the teaching plan, called simple model rotation.

Chapter 6

Phase III: Simple Model Rotation

Planning

Simple Model Rotation

The first phase of the reflective teaching and learning model revealed that the students' initial perspectives of service users showed a tendency to stereotype or categorize them. Argyris and Schön (1996: 93) saw the need to stereotype as a defensive action emanating from Model I non-reflective thinking. Also, the students had discussed the difficulties they encountered with service users as being primarily caused by poor treatment at the hands of other professionals or service providers, unreasonable behaviour on the part of the parents or a combination of the two.

I now wanted to see if it were possible to help the students develop a new, more considered outlook on service users, one that moved away from the typification of the earlier session. I also wanted to see if the students could develop a perspective on parents that included a view of themselves within the professional/service user interaction. This would allow them to advance from viewing parental reaction as always being caused by outside factors. It should also enable them to begin to appreciate the nuances of their own practice and to judge how it might impact on the relationship they were able to achieve with parents. I hypothesized that the previous phase of the teaching and learning model, which had exposed the students to the views of two parents, would have precipitated some new thoughts on what it might be like to care for a child with a disability. I considered it important to capitalize on any new developments in awareness the students might have made as a result of meeting the parents. I wanted, at this point in the research, to provide a critical learning environment in which the students could be enabled to foster such new awareness and to try to apply it to their own practice.

From this point onwards in the research, I needed to develop the classroom as a reflective practicum – a place where the students could experiment with new ideas and concepts in their work with service users. My aim was not to 'teach' such new ideas, but rather try and provide an environment in which the students could develop their ideas and test out new approaches in their practice. Dewey described this type of learning as one where the student:

> has to *see* on his own behalf and in his own way the relations between means and methods employed and results achieved. Nobody else can see for him, and he can't

see just by being 'told', although the right kind of telling may guide his seeing and thus help him see what he needs to see (Dewey 1974: 151).

One of the challenges I now faced was being able to accomplish Dewey's 'right kind of telling' which would enable the students to 'see' new perspectives, approaches and opportunities and to test them out for themselves. I considered that the continuation and development of reflective exercises and critical questioning might facilitate such learning to occur.

Summary of Purposes of Phase III

• To enable the students to develop new perspectives towards the parents with whom they work.
• To continue to implement the reflective teaching and learning model by introducing the notion of 'simple model rotation' to help students achieve a state of critically reflective learning.

Action

Using Simple Model Rotation

In this cycle of the research I began to introduce my concept of simple model rotation. This type of model rotation is characterized by 'mirroring', enabling one individual (professional) to see a situation or interaction from the standpoint of another (service user). This was done through the use of an exercise that I had developed with the help of a group of parents of disabled children. During my work with these parents they had compiled a list of the words that they felt best described the professionals who had worked with them. As a way of helping these service users to reflect on their own relationship with professionals, I then reversed the exercise and asked the parents to think how professionals might perceive parents. This generated a lively and productive debate that the parents appeared to enjoy. In his written evaluation of the session, one parent remarked: '*I got a lot out of thinking about how we might look to professionals and vice versa, made me think a lot. Hope you do it in reverse with professionals.*' This work with the parents' group on parents/professional perceptions subsequently became the foundation of my 'mirroring exercise'.

Observation

Mirroring Exercise

The students were told that, in my work with a group of service users, a number of parents had produced a list of words which they used to describe professionals.

The students were then asked to guess which words they felt parents might have chosen to use in connection with professionals. The object of this approach was to get the professionals to imagine what professionals look like from the parents' perspective and then to analyse what aspects of the professional demeanour cause parents to perceive them in particular ways. In this way the professionals become a mirror to themselves, using the mirror to rotate 180° into the parents' position and seeing what they look like from the parents' perspective (see Figure 6.1).

Figure 6.1 Simple Model Rotation

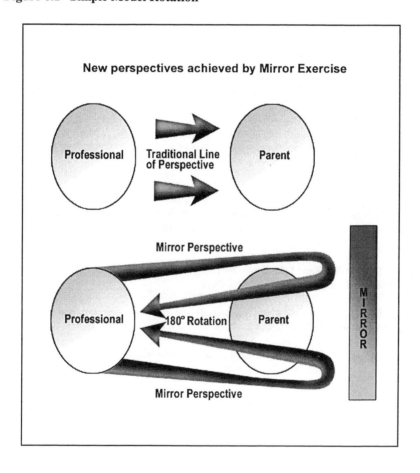

I started the exercise by asking the students to suggest what words the service users had chosen to describe professionals in order to help them begin to look at themselves from the parents' perspective.

> Researcher: I would like you to try standing in the parents' shoes and imagine what you, the professional, may look like to the parent.

Some class members had difficulty with the concept of the exercise and could not make the mirror rotation. They stayed with their own professional viewpoint and started to use words that described parents.

> Doctor: Confused.
>
> Researcher: Parents see professionals as confused?
>
> Doctor: No, the parents are confused, they can be removed from reality and sometimes they're a bit defensive because they think we're critical of them.

This student found it hard to use the mirror concept in order to 'see' the professional from the parents' position. I tried to re-frame the exercise to make it more comprehensible.

> Researcher: OK, I'm more interested in what you think parents see in *you* that makes them feel that way. If these parents seem to be behaving defensively towards professionals, what do you think they see in those professionals which make them feel like that?
>
> Family Support Worker: I think they feel they're being checked out, like we don't think they are doing a good enough job.
>
> Researcher: Can you say what professionals may look like to them, when parents experience those emotions?
>
> Family Support Worker: Em ... like they are judging the parents ... judgemental, they may see professionals as judgemental.

Albeit tentatively, this student has achieved 180° simple model rotation. From her initial comment that parents '*feel they are being checked out*', she has rotated the parental model until she saw, from the service users' perspective, that the professional may seem to be judging them.   The exchange shown above, demonstrated that adopting a reflective stance is not always easy and that the development of a critical view of established beliefs remains challenging for some students. I needed to be careful to construct a reflective environment that consistently encouraged such perspective transformation. I also needed to be vigilant for students who found the approach more difficult and who, as a consequence, might become distanced from the rest of the class.

Other group members were more adept at the exercise and managed 180° rotation with ease:

Nurse:　　　　I think we're seen as experts, as all-knowing.

Occupational Therapist:　We look detached from what may be really bothering the parents.

Psychologist:　I think we look like pushy friends – you know we have an agenda – we want to be their friends but, by the way, we also want them to do what *we* want.

Researcher:　　Can the parents see this 'other agenda' which may lie behind your friendliness?

Psychologist:　Some do and maybe they accept it as the rules of the game, but others just see you as a genuinely nice person and maybe it's pretty shocking for them to find out that we have our own professional strategy going on all the time.

This last speaker demonstrated an ability to begin to rotate her model of service users; to see aspects of herself through their eyes. She was able to stand in the parents' place and see herself initially as a caring person. By returning to her own position she acknowledged that she also had specific plans for the parents and she admitted that her display of concern could be a way of getting parents to agree to what she wished them to do. Schön (1983: 300) defines this behaviour as a constituent part of a Model I approach, where the professional conveys a sense of warmth and sympathy as a 'sweetener', but continues to maintain a distant, expert role with the client. Although this behaviour relates to Model I, the student's ability to explore the situation displays Model II attributes. She demonstrated awareness of her tacit behaviour with its inconsistencies and she was able to explore its consequences for parents. Her ability to rotate this situation suggested that she was already going beyond the 180° rotation into more complex re-positioning of the parental model which included her own role in the interchange.

Is Anything Going on at Home?

Bernie, one of the psychologists in the class, brought up a problem she had been encountering in her work. She expressed concern about a tendency she had observed in fellow professionals to assume that, if an individual with disability displayed difficult behaviour, this behaviour must relate to something occurring in the family home. She considered that this professional attitude might make parents feel like they were to blame for their young adult's behaviour.

Bernie: It's transmitted to the parents that they are hiding something, concealing something, something is going on which they are not sharing – these messages really undermine parents.

Although Bernie had identified a situation in which other professionals created a difficult situation for parents, she was able to present the issue from the rotated, parental perspective. A large proportion of the class seemed to agree with her proposition that when professionals ask, '*is anything going on at home*', it may cause service users to suspect that professionals doubt their ability to cope. However one of the students, Monica, who had been having some difficulties with the mirroring exercise, seemed to become irritated by the psychologist's ideas.

Monica: But we're trying to help the child, that's our job to understand the child. It's not a question of hurting the parents' feelings, if they care about their child and their child is behaving chaotically in their day service then I have the right to see if something is happening at home. They can't think we are invading their privacy if they care about the child.

This student was insisting that the professionals must do their job in the best interest of this individual with disability, and that their parents should appreciate the work of the professionals in this regard. She added a twist by saying that if parents loved their child enough, they would want what is best for him or her, implying that 'the best' must involve their compliance with professional expertise. Monica's perception of parental behaviour seemed to indicate a particular theory-in-use: 'good' parents will want the best for their child with disability; professionals' expertise is the best for their child; therefore parents who object to professional intervention may not be good parents. Monica subsequently suggested that parents who reject professional involvement could also be potential abusers of their children. By doing so she seemed to be 'sealing' her theory-in-use – not only are defensive parents bad, but they might also be dangerous. The single-loop aspect of her theory suggested that an unwillingness to work with professionals might indicate that parents have something to hide, so professional monitoring of such parents becomes more necessary. I checked if this represented her thinking, as such an attitude concurs with Argyris and Schön's (1996: 93) Model I action strategies that are 'protect yourself, blame others, create stereotypes, intellectualize'.

Monica: It's a very fuzzy line, it's very difficult to be one hundred percent sure that these families are not abusing their children. We know they are more likely – you have to be suspicious.

Researcher: Can I check out something with you? Did I understand you right that you feel that parents who object to professionals wanting information or access to their family might be more likely to be potential abusers?

Monica: I'm not saying they are more likely, but there would be a high index of suspicion in that those with disability are more susceptible to abuse.

Researcher: So, would you be more likely to keep an eye on such families?

Monica: Yes, from the point of view of our responsibility as carers, we have to check, they shouldn't mind if they are interested in their child's welfare, they shouldn't be defensive.

Bernie, the psychologist who had broached the issue, reintroduced a 'mirroring' of the parents' feeling.

Bernie: If somebody asked me that about my child I'd be very defensive. If I was coming to that situation I'd need to see it from the parent's point of view and then see how these parents may feel to have a social worker or a psychologist coming to their house. I know I'd hate it.

Monica: But are your children having troubles? You need to see it in that context.

Psychologist: But it's the pressure that gets put on you as a parent – the pressure we professionals put on parents. We presume to take away parental rights because we think we know better at the end of the day.

Monica: Nobody says we know better, but in the issue of sexual abuse we do know better. If you really know and love your child you should be happy to let those who work with him know if something is happening at home. There really is no need to become defensive.

Bernie was continuing to rotate the model around to what it might feel like to be in the parents' shoes, to offer the other student a chance to see different aspects of the situation. She was presenting a double-loop scenario seeking to test out the parents' perceptions of the situation, to see if that would effect the theory-in-use that was presenting. Also, having rotated the parental model and having argued from the parents' perspective, she had changed using the term 'them' to 'us' in her original reference to professionals who treat parents insensitively.

However, I realized at this point that the discussion with Monica had continued too long and, in the light of the conflicting models being presented by other students, I had not guarded against Monica becoming distanced from the rest of the class. I began to see that Monica might now feel constrained to defend her position and any prolongation of the discussion would be unprofitable, as well as potentially damaging for her.

This interchange also uncovered a fundamental issue for me. In my interchange with Monica I also recognized my own frustration with what I perceived as her inability or unwillingness to try and rotate the parental perspective. Such frustration indicated that I was in danger of pushing students towards my own way of thinking and of seeing students who could not or would not work reflectively as being weaker, or less successful than others. I considered this realization important for my future development of the reflective teaching and learning model. It will be discussed more fully in the reflection component of this phase, at the end of this chapter.

Judging the Professional

Angela, a senior nurse, presented a problem that she was encountering with parents of a man with a learning disability who resided in the agency where she worked. When this man's parents visited him, they took him into a room, examined the name-tags on his clothing and then checked if his toenails had been cut and his hair had been combed. This had been a regular occurrence for the previous fifteen years.

The class started to discuss why this continued to happen. Angela initially described the parents as *'judgemental and defensive'*, an attitude she felt they adopted because they might be questioning her ability to care for their son. Her assessment suggested that she placed the parents into the 'grateful clients' category, where ambivalence or dissatisfaction shown by parents to professional opinion could be classed as defensiveness.

> Angela:　　　Working with these particular parents, they very much judged me, taking over their role and they made me feel like I wasn't doing it as well as they could.

Prompted by me, the students applied simple model rotation to the situation, discussing what in the professional demeanour might cause this parental response. This could also be seen as double-loop testing, seeking for different rationales for the parents' behaviour.

> Researcher:　　What do you think these parents are feeling? What is their perception of you and other staff that leads them to do this?
>
> Angela:　　　Perhaps they see me as inefficient or untrustworthy.
>
> Nurse:　　　Maybe they feel guilty?
>
> Researcher:　　Well if they are, what may be happening to make them feel guilty? How do you look to them?
>
> Nurse;　　　Maybe they are embarrassed, I mean they may feel that you are better able to look after their son, that could be really hard for them.

This last speaker has now reversed Angela's original rationale for the parent's actions. She suggested to Angela that the parents might find her care of their son too efficient, rather than slipshod. Others continue this line of thinking:

Psychologist: Maybe these parents are taking over their mothering and fathering roles again when they do the checking. Like they re-claim their son.

Angela: It just seems to show such a lack of trust, if their child is in care with us then they have to hand over some trust to the people who actually look after him.

Nurse: I think they feel their son is vulnerable and it's their way of checking and saying '*I love you and I'm checking that everything is alright for you*'. I think it's the only way they can show this love, for some people it's the only way they can.

Angela: Don't you think it's abnormal though?

Nurse: No actually I don't. I think that they see you as very capable of taking care of their son and they may feel threatened by your competency. I don't deny what they are doing would irritate the heart out of me, but I would have to see it from their point of view, it's their way of dealing with a hard situation.

It may well have been the last speaker's honesty about how she felt she might react to these parents which allowed Angela to begin to rotate her model of them. For the first time in the class a student has talked about understanding the parents' perspective whilst still being annoyed and frustrated by their actions. Angela had now been offered a new perspective on this model, a new way of framing the action of these parents. Schön feels that before reflection-in-action can take place, then the practitioner has to adopt a constructionist view of the reality of his/her practice (Schön 1987: 36). I now needed to check if the new construction of the parents' reality proposed by the family support worker made sense to Angela – to see if she could refocus on this new post-rotational viewpoint.

Researcher: How does that sound to you? Because you are the one that has to work with those parents again and not be driven crazy by their actions. If you stand in their shoes now, does it look any different?

Angela: I hadn't thought of it that way before, but they might feel threatened. Like, they had been doing the job of looking after this man for over twenty years and then they had to stop doing that job. So they come in and it's like they have to see if other people could be doing that job as well as or maybe better than they had been doing it. And they had been doing it well, but I suppose we don't tell them that. We kind of just expect them to fit in now with our ways of doing things.

Social Worker: I know what you're saying, I see it all the time. When parents look at us it's can look like we only do it because we're professionals and we're paid for it, but parents know that they have to do it all the time. It's not like they are looking for credit, but nobody acknowledges it. Sometimes older parents will say '*it's so much easier on younger parents*' – they don't really mean they begrudge these other parents, but it's like they had to work so much harder and nobody noticed.

What began to emerge in the above dialogue was the number of students who demonstrated the ability to rotate the parent model. This maintenance of a reflective stance had allowed them to connect with possible new meanings for the behaviour of the parents in Angela's case. Through guided discussion Angela moved from seeing the parents as judgemental and mistrusting, to hypothesizing that the parents might be attempting to re-establish a parenting role for themselves with their son, albeit in a manner which has created barriers between them and the staff. Other students had also worked with Angela in rotating the model and, in doing so, they demonstrated a capacity for reflective reasoning. Mezirow (1990a: 10) saw such a shift in meaning perspective as central to critical reflection – 'our greatest assurance of objectivity comes from exposing an expressed idea to rational and reflective discourse'. In this case the discourse came from within the class itself and, working collectively, this group of students completed simple model rotation. By doing so they also offered Angela a new perspective which might help her in her future work with these parents who had become severely distanced from professionals taking care of their son.

At the end of this third session ended I asked the students to complete a simple exercise in their work over the following two weeks. She asked the class to take one parent or family with whom they worked, to acknowledge the opinions they hold about that family, and to note them down. Having done so, the class were asked to think about what it might be like to be in those parents' shoes and to note down any alternative perspectives which could also apply to these parents.

This 'alternative viewpoints' exercise was also given to encourage the students to continue the notion of model rotation within their practice. I thought it important to give the students simple exercises to use in the workplace between classroom sessions in order to help them to maintain a reflective outlook and to connect it to their everyday practice, rather than associating it only with work in the practicum. In this way the lessons of the practicum could be extended into the workplace and also the experiences in the workplace could be brought back into the practicum. This two-way flow of experiences was important for helping the students to appreciate their growing ability to be reflective as a transferable skill with value in different spheres of their work.

Reflection and Re-planning

'Re-seeing' Parents

This cycle of research revealed a considerable ability on the part of many of the students to sustain a reflective position in their discussion of parents. In analysing the data I looked for any references to students referring to what they, or other professionals, looked like from the parents' point of view. Of the nineteen students, fifteen made at least one reference to this rotated perspective. Almost three-quarters of these post-rotational perspectives referred to the professionals either as 'we' or 'I'. Most referred to themselves in an unflattering light:

Nurse: We look very distant.

Nurse: We seem like we're not really interested in what's bothering them.

Psychologist: We must look like we're so in control.

Such comments were important on two counts. Firstly, rather than referring to a professional in a generalized sense, the model rotation concept seemed to enable students to place themselves centrally within the interaction. Secondly, through model rotation, they also saw the potentially problematic aspects of their own practice. Some students were using the exercise to re-examine how aspects of their work routines could be interpreted quite differently by parents. This was shown in comments such as:

Nurse: You know something like a psychological assessment is so run of the mill to us, but parents take it as a life or death test for their child – you kind of forget that.

Nurse: If you were busy you would be really limited in the time you would spend with them [parents], from their point of view – that could be hard if they needed time to work up to saying what was worrying them.

This is an important change from the students' earlier tendency to focus on relationships between parents and other professionals rather than themselves and their perception that potential problems between parents and professionals were caused by other, 'insensitive' professionals. I had devised the simple model rotation exercise in order to foster the students' awareness of their theories-in-use and to help them to make explicit the implicit meaning systems that they might impose on parents.   Mezirow (1990a: 13) noted that until meaning systems were acknowledged and transformed, perspective transformation could not occur. The exercise appeared to provide many the students with a non-threatening way to re-assess some tacit work practices and to explore some relatively simple changes that could be made to accommodate a new perspective on parents.

Five of the students in the class had not accomplished the mirroring exercise by the end of this session. Two of them had remained very quiet during the session and three others had consistently discussed issues from a linear perspective of the parents. In other words, they always described the parents from the professional viewpoint. I had to consider that some students or practitioners may be either cognitively unable to achieve such a reflective state or they may just choose not to do so, no matter what type of reflective learning environments had been created.

Labouvie-Vief and Blanchard-Fields (1984: 179) explain that some adults who fail to achieve tasks associated with the acquisition of psychological autonomy may enter adulthood with rigid and highly defended thought patterns. If that is so, then there may be students in the class who will not be able, at any stage, to perform model rotation, creating a situation in which such students could remain bewildered by their classmates' intellectual activities.   There could also be students who considered the reflective exercises irrelevant or unsuitable for their professional needs. In that case, it would be their choice not to participate in the work of the researcher. In either case I would have to be careful to monitor such students' future participation and to guard against them becoming isolated within the class.

A noticeable change had occurred between those students using a rotated parental perspective and those maintaining a linear perspective. The students who completed model rotation also appeared to have stopped categorizing parents. For example, in Angela's analysis of the parents who continually needed to check on their son's well-being, her original assessment of the situation was inclined to label the parents as judgemental. However after model rotation, her perspective on the family indicated that she appreciated the uniqueness of the parents' situation: '*They come in and it's like they have to see if other people could be doing that job as well as they had been doing it. And they had been doing it well, but I suppose we don't tell them that.*' In this statement she moved towards seeing these service users as individuals. However the two students who had not rotated the parents' model, made comments about '*the parents' lack of trust*' and a '*lack of gratitude towards the professionals*'. In contrast, none of the other students who discussed the case post-rotationally labelled the parents' behaviour as pathological, nor did they question a lack of gratitude on the service users' behalf. This indicates that by rotating the parental model, students seemed less likely to engage in typification, confirming Mezirow's (1991: 16) theory that typification is characteristic of non-reflective thinking.

Reviewing My Own Perspective

In relation to my own positioning in the research, I also had to acknowledge and analyse the argument that developed between myself and Monica. When Monica appeared to 'refuse' to complete model rotation, my initial reaction was to become angry with her and to argue points, which proved ultimately frustrating for both of us. I had to remind myself that it was not my role to 'persuade' students to reflect, but to provide them with the best possible reflective environment. The choice to become reflective ultimately remained solely with the students. I also reflected that a number of students in the class were from what Glazier (1974: 346) called a 'hard' scientific profession, built upon technically rational principles. The environment which I was attempting to create in the classroom might, therefore, be quite alien to their experience of third-level education.

I also recognized that, during this session I had wanted to achieve a balance between allowing the class to reflect on their attitudes to parents, while ensuring that the session had coherence and direction. In reviewing the transcripts of this session I acknowledged a tendency in myself to talk too much, to try to 'control' the interaction. An analysis of my own contributions during the session also revealed an inclination to 'push' discussions forward and not to leave enough periods of silence to allow students to develop issues at their own speed. I had to accept the need to monitor this issue in my own performance and to resist the tendency to interrupt or urge students inappropriately.

Future Planning

I now wanted to move on to more complex levels of reflection. This third cycle of action had yielded data which indicated that fifteen students (just over three quarters of the class) were able to complete simple model rotation, thus appreciating some of the aspects of the parents' standpoint. The next stage was to explore if the students could recognize these new perspectives in their own work and to challenge them to reflectively analyse aspects of their own direct practice with parents. This next step would be called full model rotation.

Chapter 7

Phase IV: Full Model Rotation

Planning

The previous action research cycles had demonstrated that, through the reflective teaching model, most of the students were becoming increasing able to achieve simple model rotation – specifically seeing themselves and their professional persona from the service users' perspective. This degree of model rotation had begun to introduce students to a new level of reflection that made it less likely for them to accept an 'easy', one-dimensional, technically rational explanation of parents' attitudes and behaviour. I now wanted to capitalize on this increase in their reflective capabilities to address certain key issues. Could professionals identify their own tacit attitudes towards service users through a reflective analysis of their own practice? Also, could the evolving teaching and learning model continue to help professionals identify more effective and equitable practice approaches in their own work?

Achieving Full Model Rotation

At this point I was interested in expanding the rotation of the service user perspective that the students were undertaking. If my design of simple model rotation had offered students a 180° 'turn' on their perspective of service users, my ideas for full model rotation should now allow them to 'turn and revolve' their view of the service user a full 360° (see Figure 7.1). I proposed achieving this 'turn and revolution' by working with the students in such a way as to allow them to 'walk around' an interaction they had experienced with a service user and to re-see that interaction from a more reflective perspective. A vital element of full model rotation is the student's ability to include themselves in the fully rotated model and to be able to stand back from their work with service users and critically analyse their own role in the professional/service user interaction. Figure 7.1 reveals how the professional/service user interchange is changed from being one that is only perceived from the professional's point of view. In full model rotation, through the help of reflective teaching approaches, the professional becomes able to rotate the interchange between themselves and the service user, thus providing them with an unlimited number of new perspectives on how the interaction has progressed.

Figure 7.1   Full Model Rotation

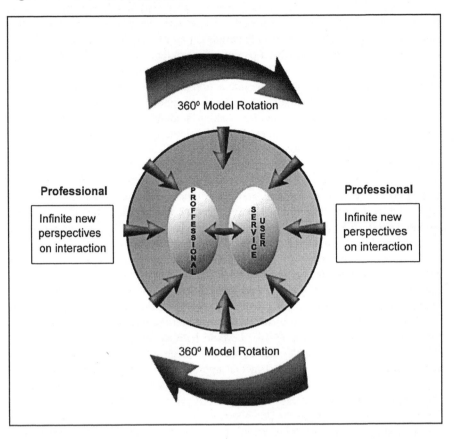

Full model rotation requires students to work at a more evolved level of reflection. It allows them to move from their more immediate tacit reactions to service users, and to develop more reflective, considered views of how they function within their own practice. I speculated that full model rotation should result in students being able to recognize tacit aspects of their professional practice and to analyse the effectiveness of some of their current practice approaches. By helping students to critically re-see a piece of their own work, full model rotation could also help them develop longer-term reflective attitudes to their work which would then become an integral part of their practice.

Preparing the Case Studies

In order to help the students to achieve full model rotation, I drew on Argyris and Schön's (1974, 1996) action theory as discussed in Chapter 3. As stated already, in order to more closely involve students in the analysis of their own work, I had simplified Argyris and Schön's diagnostic model to fit more closely into the my own research design. As Argyris and Schön (1992: xxii) had done with more than five thousand individuals over a period of more than twenty-five years, I asked the students to prepare a short case study based on part of a challenging intervention or issue they had encountered with a parent. The students were asked to divide their case studies into an account of the dialogue that occurred, augmented by a record of their own internal thoughts as the interaction progressed. By asking the students to record both spoken dialogue and internal thoughts, I intended that this task in itself would be a reflective exercise. Asking students to recall and record their unspoken opinions during the interaction was aimed at encouraging them to begin to rotate the parental perspectives. Argyris and Schön's method of case study preparation bears a close resemblance to the process recording used in social work which Papell and Skolnick (1992: 23) see as an important tool for stimulating reflection in social work students and practitioners. The preparation of this case study and its presentation to the class provided a baseline for each student to begin to fully rotate their perception of the service user, starting from their original perception of the service user at the beginning of the interaction.

My role in this phase of the teaching and learning model was to create a reflective environment, primarily through minimal reflective prompts and questions, in which the group could present and examine their individual case studies. By doing so they could begin to acknowledge their initial perception of the service users and the aims with which they entered the interaction. In Argyris and Schön's phraseology (1996: 13-14), I would help students look at their espoused theory or explicit rationale for a specific piece of work and to note any inconsistency between it and their actual approach to their work – their theory-in-use. Thus this exercise was aimed at helping the students to begin examining any dichotomies between what they set out to achieve in their work with parents and what ultimately occurred in the practice environment. The professionals were also challenged to specify their perception of the parents at the start of the interaction and to note how this perception aided or hampered the work they subsequently attempted. Lastly the students were encouraged to reflect upon how successful their espoused theory had been in achieving their perceived goals in the interaction with the parent/s.

A specific aspect of Argyris and Schön's action theory which I chose to simplify was the language and the complexity of the analytic model which they used to diagnose espoused theory and theory-in-use. I wanted to offer the students a way of examining and understanding the tacit aspects of their own practice so that they could begin to acknowledge how these affected their work. To do so, I developed a new and less complex analytical formula to facilitate examination of the case studies. This new analytic formula asked students to answer four reflective questions on the case they were presenting – a framework that I called the Four-Question Case Audit, herein after referred to as the 4.Q.C.A. (see Figure 7.2).

I developed the 4.Q.C.A. to give the students a relatively simple analytic tool which they could not only apply to the case study they presented in class, but one which they could also learn to use easily in their own practice. Looking at Argyris and Schön's analyses of their students' case studies (1974: 37-138; 1996: 122-149), they were based on the relatively complex framework for diagnosing theory-in-use (Figure 6.1). However, in practice, Argyris and Schön did not offer their student practitioners this complex model as a means of analysing their work. Instead the authors assisted the students through an analysis of their cases, primarily using their model as a guide for themselves rather than as a general tool for the use of all participants. As noted in Chapter 3, this left Argyris and Schön open to the criticism of maintaining a degree of mastery and mystery within their own practice, even when working towards removing such tendencies in the practice of others. I designed the framework for case analysis (the 4.Q.C.A.) to have more transparency, in which the students would be included and involved in all steps of the reflective teaching and learning model.

Figure 7.2 Four-Question Case Audit (4.Q.C.A.)

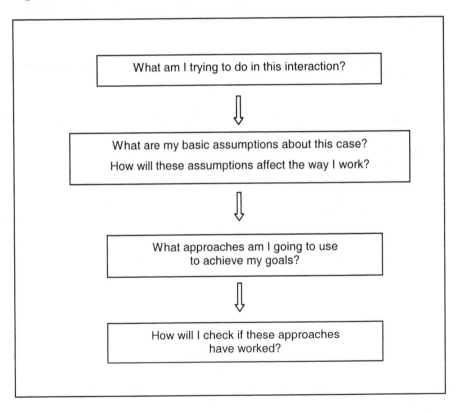

Argyris and Schön (1974: 38-39) advised that the students' diagnoses of their theories in action must be pursued in an atmosphere which allows participants to reveal their behaviour to themselves and to others without needing to adopt defensive or self-protective behaviour. I needed to sustain a class environment in which levels of trust could be developed among the students themselves and between the students and myself. As noted in the previous phase of the teaching and learning model, there were five students who had not yet practiced simple model rotation and care was needed in monitoring these and any other students who might feel intimidated or distanced from the process. To this end I reviewed the tapes of each class shortly after it ended and observed each student's contribution in terms of general participation in class discussion with specific reference to rotated perspectives.

The final aspect of the planning for this phase of the reflective teaching and learning model was to familiarize the students with the concept of Model I and Model II practice as an adjunct to their work on the case studies. Argyris and Schön (1992: xix) noted that reflecting on action theory and theory-in-use is a prerequisite for improving professional performance, especially the acquisition of Model II – reflective practice. The authors (1992: xxiii) believe that it is necessary for learners to be able to compare their practice with the concepts inherent in Model I and II practice.

Summary of the Purposes of Phase IV of the Teaching and Learning Model

- To continue the reflective work begun in the previous three cycles, especially the development of new and more complex views of service users that had been made possible through simple model rotation.
- To introduce an analytic framework to help students to analyse their own practice in as effective and productive a manner as possible, also familiarizing students with the concepts of Model I and Model II behaviour in practice.
- To use such a framework in the classroom in a way which allowed students to become familiar with its concepts and to encourage them to use the framework as a means of self-analysis of practice perspectives in the future.
- To use the framework in a way which produced minimal defensiveness, to monitor students who might find the reflective approach difficult or irrelevant and to guard against them becoming distanced from the process.

Action

Preparing to Present Cases

The next eight hours of class time were taken up by the students' presentations of case studies from their practice, to which they applied the 4.Q.C.A. Guidelines given to the class for preparing their case studies had suggested that they should choose a practice incident that represented a challenging intervention or issue that they had encountered with a parent. The guidelines placed no limits on the subject selected, but proposed that it should relate to a problem or issue which was central to the student's relationship with the service user/s. Although I had anticipated that full model rotation might occur during the analysis of these case studies, as will be seen later, the preparation of this case study also precipitated some students to gain important new perspectives within their own practice.

Within this phase of the teaching and learning model, a variety of case studies were presented and analysed by the class. At the start of the class every student was given a copy of the particular case study being studied so that they could follow what had transpired in each interaction. Each case study presentation began with the external dialogue being read aloud, with different students reading the part of the case participants and the case presenter reading his or her own part. I used this approach because she thought it important to make each case study as 'real' as possible for the case presenter and the other students. I also felt that it was important to use the written case study as the focus of these sessions, as it gave all the students the same concrete scenario to consult, discuss and analyse.

After the reading of the case study, I asked the students to form into small groups of two or three to discuss and note their initial reactions to each case. This small-group work was designed to help all the students, particularly the ones who were less comfortable talking in the larger class, to participate as fully as possible in the exercise. This was considered particularly important at the beginning of this phase of the teaching and learning model for some of the students who had been quiet during the previous phase, making it difficult to know how they were responding to model rotation. The main part of the case analysis was promoted by the use of the 4.Q.C.A. Although I initially posed the questions in the audit, when the students became more familiar with the format of the 4.Q.C.A. they took over most of this function themselves. The case study presentations ended with a general class discussion, which were designed to encourage the students to identify common themes emerging as more case material was discussed.

My role as researcher/teacher in this phase of the development of the teaching and learning model was to continue to use minimal prompts and critical questions to promote a reflective atmosphere in the class. Following my reflection on the previous phases of the model, I studied the tapes after each session in this phase in order to monitor my own contributions, watching particularly for my own Model I-type tendencies to control or dominate class discussion. I further reviewed the tapes for examples of simple model rotation that revealed incidents of students re-seeing themselves through the mirror of the parents. I also looked for examples of full model rotation, in which students demonstrated an ability to 'stand back' in a reflective manner from their work with parents and re-see the action between themselves and the parents through new perspectives.

Observation

Analysing the Case Studies

The rest of this chapter will examine some aspects of the case studies, exploring
how the students presented and analysed the interactions.

Case Study No 1. (Debbie): 'Dealing with Harry's Mother' This case relates to a
situation where a professional has become entangled in a contentious situation with
a service user, a common topic emerging from the case studies prepared by the
class. Practically all these scenarios relate to unease on the part of a parent of a
disabled adult about the professional's encouragement to allow this adult greater
freedom or independence. Such a contentious situation was epitomized by the case
of Harry, a man in his early thirties with a mild level of learning disability, who
lived in the family home. Professionals working with Harry felt that a move away
from home would be beneficial for him and they noted that Harry also appeared
keen to live more independently. Debbie, a nurse working in Harry's day service,
had been sent to discuss the matter with Harry's mother.

Debbie preceded her presentation by telling the class that she had *'got nowhere
with Harry's mother'* and she warned the class *'I did very badly here, it's pretty
embarrassing – I think I'm completely set in Model I.'* Debbie's comment has
significance because, by the time the case study analyses began, most of the class
members were comfortable in referring appropriately to Schön's models of the
technically rational and the reflective practitioner making appropriate and regular
references to Model I and Model II behaviour. It was also interesting, in terms of
judging the degree of trust that was building within the class, that Debbie appeared
comfortable in presenting a case that had not gone well for her.

Question 1
• What am I trying to do in this interaction?

As in all cases analysed, I introduced the 4.Q.C.A. by asking each case presenter to
state their overall view and their goals at the start of the interaction. Debbie felt that
her principal goal in the interaction was *'needing to persuade Harry's mother that
he was able to manage away from home'*.

> Debbie: Well, he was anxious to move out and my goal was to fight his
> corner, I guess, at all costs. I was just going in ... I thought, he's sick of it at home
> ... he has the right to move out if he chooses and maybe ... I was a bit angry that he
> was being put in the situation of having to fight for his right to leave home, that it
> was such an ordeal for him.

The initial perceptions and goals described by Debbie were common to some other
cases presented by students. In a similar case, another student felt that she had to

'*fight* [young adult with disability's] *battles, because she didn't want to stay with her family, she loved respite care*'. As in Debbie's case the student encountered considerable problems with a parents who did not share her assessment of the situation.

Question 2
- What are my basis assumptions about this situation?
- How will these assumptions affect the way I work?

The second element of the case analysis is the statement of assumptions that the professional holds about the situation prior to the interaction. I asked Debbie to articulate her original perception of the situation, recording the points she made. Debbie's initial assessment of the situation was:
- that Harry wanted to leave home;
- that his mother was defensive to new ideas;
- that his mother was restrictive in what she would allow Harry to do;
- that his mother was mistaken in her anxieties about Harry's inability to cope away from her.

Debbie's initial view of the case suggested that, because of these assumptions, her approach would have to be focused on upholding the right of the adult with learning disability in spite of his mother's wishes to the contrary. She noted '*I had to fight his corner because I saw that my responsibility was to him.*' This is a characteristic motivation in situations where the professional perceives that he/she has a very different view to the service user as how to act. In many cases the professional may then proceed to 'tell' the service user that they must change, without testing out why the service users hold such different views or, indeed if they hold these views at all. Thus the professional enters a win/lose situation with the service user, a characteristic of a Model I approach to practice.

Questions 3 & 4
- What approaches am I going to use?
- How will I check if these approaches have worked?

The third and fourth inter-linked questions relate to the chosen approaches and the professional's means of verifying their efficacy. Debbie stated that her approach was '*to persuade his mother that Harry was able to manage away from home, I guess I felt some hard truths had to be dished out to the Mum*'. She felt that she would know if her approach had been successful if '*Well, if I got her to let Harry move out of home, I'd have achieved what I wanted if ... well OK, if she stopped thinking she was right and started believing I was right, then I could have achieved what I wanted for Harry.*'

Debbie's original assessment that she was '*very Model I*' in this case appears accurate from her acknowledgement of a win/lose approach with Harry's mother.

Reflection in Action

In this and other cases in this area of intellectual disability, the win/lose element becomes more complicated because, ostensibly, the professional is not trying to win for himself or herself, but trying to win for the person with a disability. So, the need to win becomes a selfless act and, arguably, may be perceived by the professional as having greater integrity because of that. What may not be acknowledged is that the parent still remains the loser; whether they lose to a selfish or altruistic professional, the stigma of losing still remains.

Reading the Case Study

Whatever the motivation on the professional's part, it appeared in the case dialogue that Debbie began to run into difficulties when she broached the topic of Harry leaving home.

Internal Monologue	External Dialogue
I know I'm getting into a tricky area now.	*Debbie*: 'We have discussed this with Harry, where he sees himself in the future and he has expressed an interest in moving out of home. He sees it as a positive step forward in his life, something that is natural for a person at his stage.'
Here she goes!	*Mother*: 'I think it's just a fad – he wants to move out today and tomorrow he'll be quite happy to stay at home. It's just a stage he's going through because he has seen some of his friends moving out of home.'
I feel this is what she would like to believe. I need to try and explain it's more than a fad.	*Debbie*: 'Well I don't think so, he's been taking about it for some time now, even before his friends were finding flats. It's a very natural progression.'
	Mother: 'Look, it's as simple as this, I don't think that Harry would be able to look after himself. He would never take a shower, for example.'
All those things can be addressed.	*Debbie*: 'But he would still be attending the Day Centre and we would tackle all those areas before he moves out.'
	Mother: 'Yes, but I'd be up all night worrying about him and so would his father. What if something happened and he didn't come home, nobody would know.'

Fair enough, but her worries shouldn't dictate Harry's life. I have to get her around to think about Harry's rights to make his own decisions.	*Debbie*: 'OK, there are concerns, but Harry does not think that these are valid enough to determine that he continues to live at home. When you look at it from his point of view, he feels he has the right to move out.'

Debbie was clear from the outset that her interaction with Harry's mother had gone badly and she was interested in exploring why that had happened. Argyris and Schön (1974: 42) see such openness to examine perceived failures as a vital part of creating a group dynamic where learning can occur. Her willingness to reflect-on-action was also conducive to helping her to perform model rotation, as she began to alter and expand her perspectives on Harry's mother.

The group began looking at the case material and one of the students commented that, during the interview, Debbie seemed to be *'just ploughing on, regardless'*. I asked, if that was so, how this might relate to Debbie's original perspective of the situation.

Researcher: Has Debbie stayed with her perspective of Harry's mother as obstructive, restrictive and defensive through the interaction or has she tried to double-loop test the situation and see if she's correct in her assessment of this woman?

Debbie: No, I think it's all pretty much single-loop. I went in with the idea and I stayed with it, to the bitter end!

Psychologist: Yes, she seemed to hang on to the original perception of the mother and, by doing so I get the feeling that she was ploughing herself deeper and deeper into a place she couldn't get out of. You know, where I grew up when it snowed really hard you would try and shovel it all away. But sometimes it would pile up too high and it would all fall down and you would be buried in the mound, so you would have work even harder. The more you shovelled the worse it got and the further and further away you got from your goal. That's what it seems to have been like for Debbie.

Debbie: That's it, that's just what it felt like.

The psychologist's snow metaphor proved attractive to the class and they continued to use it as they discussed the case. It also proved an inventive way of looking at the problems of maintaining a static parental perspective, supported by single-loop learning. Another student took the metaphor further:

Doctor: When you were just digging yourself deeper into the snow you weren't taking account of her views at all – that's why it kept falling in on you. There was no partnership in the situation because you're not taking on her views at all. It's a very difficult situation because you feel what you're doing is right. Yet she is coming from the opposite side, so you haven't met on the middle ground, or there's no sort of compromise on either side. I'm sure she is quite right, she should be worried and is worried, you know, and she has looked after him for 34 years and knows what he's like.

Researcher: What do you think Debbie would need to have done to change her perspective of the mother?

Debbie: Oh, I know that myself. I noticed even as I was writing up the case study, I noticed when I was writing it up, it's the lack of questions on my part. I never asked this woman any questions at any stage.

Researcher: What does that indicate?

Debbie: Lack of interest in what she was thinking. I'm not interested in what she has to say, the action is all one-way.

This interchange was important on a number of counts. Debbie had shown herself to be able to complete full model rotation, not only to re-see herself through the mirror of Harry's mother, but also to 'walk-around' her interchange with Harry's mother and re-see the interaction in a new way. By fully rotating the model of her work with Harry's mother Debbie acknowledged a lack of public testing of her theories-in-use. By not asking Harry's mother any questions, she did not open herself to the option that her original perception of this woman might be incorrect. Thus, by holding on to her original perspective she had to work hard to maintain what then appeared to be a flawed position.

Debbie's seemingly simple observation about a lack of questions proved to be very useful. It sparked a class discussion on whether the willingness of the professional to ask questions might be an indicator of Model II behaviour in an interaction. It also, as will be discussed later, provided the class with a serviceable analytic tool for helping them recognize Model I and Model II behaviour in other case studies.

Researcher: How did the lack of questions affect how the interaction developed?

Debbie: It's kind of like I was playing tennis with the Mum – She hits off a problem, I reply with a solution okay, solution, problem, solution, problem. You know pretty soon you're running out of solutions.

Researcher: Can anyone say what Debbie looked like from Harry's mother's point of view at this point?

Psychologist: Someone who wasn't listening. This mother has expertise about her son and here was someone who wasn't looking for that expertise, wasn't taking it into account. By not asking questions Debbie could stay in Model I behaviour.

Nurse: Yes, like that's how you don't have to look for any alternative ways of doing things other than the one you start with. So to become Model II, you have to open yourself to new ideas and you have to ask questions to get those new ideas.

Doctor: That's interesting about the questions because, well, go back to Debbie, because she didn't ask questions, from the Mum's point of view Debbie was advocating a huge change in Harry's life but because she didn't ask for any information she looked like she hadn't thought through a lot of the implications, things that maybe only the Mum would know about.

Nurse: So the professional may need to ask questions to say to the parent '*you have expertise that I need*'.

I then asked the whole group if they would modify the original assessment of Harry's mother following this discussion. There was agreement with Debbie's original analysis that the case was '*mostly Model I*'. The group noted that the interaction had contained traditional Model I governing variables such as Debbie's unilateral definition of specific goals and the creation of a strong win/lose situation. Using Debbie's original perspective list as a basis for discussion, the group then suggested changes to the earlier perspectives of Harry's mother as defensive, restrictive and mistaken and began to create possible new perspectives of her such as:

- Harry's mother might have been in possession of important information about Harry;
- she needed to share this information and have it acknowledged;
- she was entitled to be involved in decision making about Harry's future.

Having evolved these new perspectives, there was general agreement that it would be more difficult to enter such an interaction without seeing the importance of asking questions and offering Harry's mother the chance to have her opinion heard and included in decision making. This indicates that the original 'model' of Harry's mother has been fully rotated by considering far more complex aspects of what motivated and constrained the way she reacted to Debbie's suggestions. Another case, presented later, took the students' attempts at full model rotation in a somewhat different direction.

Case Study No 2. (Carmel): 'Facing up to Parental Anger' The problems encountered by professionals facing the dissatisfaction of service users with were exemplified in the case of Carmel, an experienced nurse, and the parents of a three-year-old child named Susan.   Susan had been referred to Carmel's home-support service, because of possible developmental delays. Carmel began working with the little girl at home, helping her to start communicating through play and she also helped her parents develop new approaches to encourage Susan to begin to speak. Carmel had been working with Susan's family for a number of months and had developed a good relationship with both Susan and her parents. During this period psychological assessment was being strongly recommended for Susan by other agency personnel, but her parents were initially very reluctant to proceed with this. Carmel suspected, as it subsequently transpired, that such an assessment would reveal that Susan had autism. Soon after Susan's parents had finally agreed to and attended for psychological testing, Carmel called to see the family, to see how they had got on.

Question 1
- What am I trying to do in this interaction?

In response to the first question of the 4.Q.C.A Carmel stated that she was *'fairly sure'* that the family would have been given the diagnosis of Susan's autism and she guessed that they would be very distressed by the news. She saw that her goal in this interaction would be to offer support to the family, which she thought she would be in a good position to do as she had developed a good relationship with them in the past.

Question 2, 3 and 4
- What are my basis assumptions about this situation?
- How will these assumptions affect the way I work?
- What approaches am I going to use?
- How will I check if these approaches have worked?

As in the previous case, Carmel charted up her perceptions she had of the situation prior to meeting with the family. They included the possibilities that:

- the family would be very upset at the diagnosis;
- the family might be angered by the diagnosis;
- the family would need support;
- she (Carmel) would be well placed to help them talk about their upset.

The reading of case study revealed that Carmel was correct in her prediction of anger, but the anger was not at the diagnosis of autism, but at Carmel herself. She was met with a barrage of anger from both Susan's mother and father.

Internal Dialogue	External Dialogue
	Mother: 'I'm really annoyed with you, you should have told us that she had autism, why didn't you tell us?'

What should I say now?	*Carmel*: 'I'm very sorry if I've upset you. Yes, I did suspect that Susan had autistic tendencies. But I do not make or give diagnoses.'
	Mother: 'But you should have informed us and told us what you thought.'
She really didn't realize that Susan had a serious problem.	*Carmel*: 'In my profession, I do not make or give diagnoses. The diagnosis is not given without much consideration and is generally made by a psychologist or a psychiatrist. You know that what I've been doing with you is talking about Susan's behaviour and management.'
	Mother: 'Oh yes, but when I told you about Susan's behaviour and what she was doing now you said "*good, great*". You didn't tell us the truth and I expected you to be honest with us.'
This woman is really angry, I wish she would only listen.	*Carmel*: 'It is true that Susan has made some progress. She will now use eye contact, concentrate for short periods and is using much better self-help skills. This has to be acknowledged.'
	Father: 'You should have told us what you thought about Susan. You've been coming here for the past three months and you're the one that knows Susan best.

I asked the class, working in pairs, to look at this interaction and to begin to analyse Carmel's initial approach to the family. The students, early on, began identifying what they saw as Model I and Model II aspects of behaviour in Carmel's approach. One of the other students wondered if the parents would have been angry at anyone who was associated with the transmission of such devastating news. The teacher in the group used simple model rotation to help Carmel re-see herself from the parents' perspective.

> Teacher: Their anger was about something different – they were angry because you, Carmel, and other people knew something really important about this child and you hadn't told them. From their point of view, you knew something vital to them and did not tell them, you had let them down.

One of the nurses took up the previous student's simple rotation of the situation and began a full rotation of the interaction between Carmel and the parents.

> Nurse: Yes, because if you were a friend of hers, and you knew this, you probably would have said it to her long ago. But here you were, a nurse, and you couldn't go across the professional boundaries and tell them until there was a professional diagnosis. Because the reality is that you did know, and you had probably discussed it with the psychologist, was that the case?

Carmel: Well, I rang the psychologist before I went out to the family.

Nurse: So lots of people knew, but nobody had told the family.   And because of 'professional boundaries', because of where your profession is in the scheme of things, you couldn't have really. But the family couldn't see it that way. That looks like Model I behaviour – them and us, them and me.

This new perspective of Carmel after full model rotation does suggest that Carmel's attitude to the parents could be considered as falling within the parameters of Model I behaviour. However, as the class continued with their analysis of the case, a number of other students offered new perspectives. It became clear in discussing the case further that, following their initial anger, the family did feel able to discuss their distress with Carmel. The students also identified the previously good relationship that Carmel had with the family prior to this interaction. Carmel described this herself from the perspective of the parents, in simple model rotation.

Carmel: They found it really hard bringing Susan to clinics because she was so disruptive. For them I think they liked that I came to the house, in a discreet way, nobody knew I was there, I wasn't in uniform. I think I didn't really seem like a 'professional' to them.

Nurse: So they had learned to trust you, I think that's really important in how you were able to work with them. But if you had to wear a uniform, like I do, then it's hard to stop being just 'the nurse'.

Psychologist: But maybe the uniform is symbolic as well as real. Like we want to 'put on a uniform' without really doing so, when we're getting into a Model I state … does that make sense?

One of the important facets of a Model II relationship is that it is based on the concept of the sharing of valid information. The class seemed to be in agreement that Carmel had already established a reflective, Model II relationship with this family. The students discussed the possibility that when the parents received information that they suspected Carmel already had and had not shared with them, this conflicted with the type of relationship they felt they had established with her. The parents' anger with her then becomes more understandable and her temporary lapse into Model I behaviour could be accounted for as a reaction to the intensity of their anger.

Using the metaphor of 'putting on a uniform' to denote occasions when one adopts a professional facade, proved attractive to other students. A number of students found it easy to understand and nine of the students referred to the metaphor appropriately in their contribution to the case analysis during the session. This concurs with Schön's belief (1979: 254) that when metaphors are used appropriately, they allow new levels of reflection to occur.

In the analysis of Carmel's case study it was possible to recognize a professional with a well-developed sense of reflection in her practice, capable of appreciating a number of complex perspectives on this family. Although the initial presentation of the case might have suggested a lack of congruence between her espoused theory and her theory-in-use, Carmel did enter the interaction attempting to support Susan's family, an objective which she seems to have been trying to achieve in her earlier dealings with them. However, the family's reaction to her, after their initial anger, indicates that they did have a relationship based on trust and shared information, and she was able to begin to re-instate that relationship with them. Model rotation in this case offered Carmel a way of reinterpreting the parents' anger towards her. It also offered her a way re-seeing herself in her work with the parents that highlighted her importance to them.

Having rotated the parental model Carmel raised the difficulty for her of knowing that Susan had autism and the problems of being within a professional system which precluded her from discussing it with the family.

Carmel: When you start to look at how it might have felt for the parents, they had their own suspicions but maybe they kept looking to me to get clues. When I said nothing then they could convince themselves that Susan was OK. On a previous visit the Dad kept saying 'it's all just a storm in a teacup' but I didn't, I couldn't, tell him it wasn't so. At the end of that session, I said to them: '*Do you not want me to come back anymore?*' And they said, '*Oh yes, we want you, but we don't want a speech therapist and we don't want to go to clinics. But we do want you ...*'

Researcher: Do you think this was indicative of how important you were to them?

Carmel: Yes, but I let them build up defences, I didn't stop them, then they may have felt that I allowed them to convince themselves that their daughter was OK.

An important aspect of Carmel's case is that her previously good relationship with the family could be compromised by the organizational system within which she worked. Up to this point the reflective teaching and learning model had explored the ways of facilitating reflective practice within the individuals being studied – how to foster Model II behaviour in individuals more used to working within a Model I mind-set. What now began to emerge was an obstacle to reflective practice which existed within the larger organizational system – the problem of fostering Model II behaviour with those who work within a system which may be, by its nature, Model I. Continuing the earlier metaphor, Carmel may have been forced by her organizational structure to appear in uniform – to withhold her own opinions in deference to professionals higher in the professional hierarchy.

Carmel was not alone in presenting case material that showed the student as being constrained by their work system. For example, another case involved a parent who, incensed by the poor service offered by her son's residential agency, targeted her anger at the direct-care staff on his unit. A further case dealt with parents in a state of distress over the lack of service provision for their young child. In these cases model rotation led both students to see that their work and their ability to respond in an honest fashion was constrained by their agency. As one of these students commented: '*How can you be Model II with service users when the system both you and they are in is Model I?*' This issue will be examined further in the next chapter.

Reflection and Re-planning

The cases discussed in this chapter are representative of many of the issues and debates which transpired over the penultimate phase of the reflective teaching and learning model. The students' ability to rotate their views of service users became more evident as the classes continued, as did the ease with which all the students used the criteria of Model I and Model II practice as a point of reference for case analysis. By the final session in which the cases were presented I had recorded that all students had made at least two attempts at model rotation.

Phase IV of the reflective teaching and learning model produced a number of important elements. Firstly the construction and utilization of metaphors, including Rose's 'snow' metaphor for a professional becoming overwhelmed in a hostile interaction with a parent and Carmel's 'uniform' metaphor as a reference to technically rational behaviour. Such metaphors and their adoption by the students in general evolved from a growing ability within the class to look for and to find more ways to express and examine elements in their practice. Also, as these metaphors were constructed within the class, they also offered students ways of rotating the model of their own practice that was unique to their own group.

A second important element was the suggestion that the presence of questions in an interaction might be an indication of a Model II approach in practice. The students tested out this hypothesis in subsequent cases and found that, in cases where no questions were asked, the professional tended to end the interaction in a more hostile manner with the parent/s. In cases where a number of questions were asked the case tended to end with more agreement between parent and professional. Three of the students chose to monitor their own level of questioning in on-going work situations undertaken during this phase of the research and they reported that ensuring a level of questions in an interaction seemed to improve their level of communication with others. By doing this all three students were demonstrating reflection-in-action.

A growing level of trust in the class marked this phase of the research. Brookfield considers a successfully reflective teacher can have a positive effect on how trust can be engendered.

> A teacher who takes students seriously shows that she can be trusted. A teacher who emphasizes peer learning shows that it is important to trust other students. A teacher who encourages students to point out to her anything about her action that is

oppressive and who seeks to change what she does, in response to their concerns, is a model of critical reflection (Brookfield 1995: 26).

This trust also seems to engender the emergence of a 'blurring' of professional roles. In the early weeks of the research comments such as *'I don't usually have much to do with parents because I'm a nurse'* or *'You would be more used to that as a social worker'* were recorded. This professional differentiation became much less obvious in the latter sessions. It was especially noticeable that the students who were nurses became more confident in voicing opinions and challenging the views of those who would be considered higher in the professional power structure, especially doctors and psychologists. As the students attended other classes together, it would be unfair to claim that such changes emerged purely as a result of their exposure to this reflective methodology. However, a growing sense of equity in the class became evident as the weeks progressed, along with a willingness to reveal practice dilemmas for class discussion. The effect of the group dynamic on the reflective methodology will be examined in the next chapter.

As my time with the class neared completion, I discussed with the students how they would like to end their sessions. Before the end of the penultimate group it was agreed that the final session would be given over to an evaluation of all their work together over the previous seven months. It was decided to take this feedback partly in the form of a written questionnaire and augmented by a group discussion. The next chapter deals with the feedback taken at this final session and also develops some overall findings emerging from the work with the class.

Chapter 8

Phase V: Ending the Research

This chapter looks at specific issues that emerged both for me and the students as my time with the class drew to a close. It explores the students' evaluation of their seven-month experience of reflective teaching and also look at some specific issues that began to emerge at the end of the research. This chapter also contains my own reflections on my experiences through the research as a whole, and it also examines different issues that emerged for me during consultative sessions with two 'critical friends' during the course of the research.

Identifying Patterns of Reflective Change

Previous chapters have outlined the changes within the group of students in different sessions, including their growing abilities to explore more complex aspects of the parents with whom they were working. I also examined general, observable changes over the course of the research. A further aim was to assess whether it was possible to identify any specific points in the practicum at which significant perspective transformation had occurred. Using Atlas.TI (a computer-based system for qualitative data analysis), I searched for noticeable qualitative changes in the students' discussion of parents and their own professional practice. This analysis revealed two major shifts in the character of observations about parents made by the students during the course of the research. The first shift in parental perspectives was recorded after the parents' session and during the first application of the mirroring exercise. The second shift occurred during the latter stages of the presentation of case studies.

Period One: Generalization of Service Users

Looking at the transcripts of the classes it was noticeable that, at the start of the research, the students tended to talk in quite generalized terms about service users, discussing them at somewhat of a remove from the professional. The first major qualitative differences in their observations about parents were recorded during and after session two, when the class worked with Tess and Suzanne, the two parents. In her evaluation of this session one of the students noted that *'this session was really powerful for me, I had never really thought about what those women were discussing'*. Another student reported that she *'felt really guilty after meeting the parents, but that class was a real turning point for me'*.

This reference to the parents' session as being a 'turning point' relates to an important element in the process of critical reflection or transformatory learning – discovering a precipitating event that triggers a significant change in perspective. While Mezirow notes that such precipitating events can take many forms (1991: 87), Brookfield describes 'trigger events' which cause discomfort of perplexity, which lead to a phrase of appraisal and self-examination (1987: 26-28). As has already been noted in Chapter 5, the students rated the parent's session very highly. They used words such as *'thought provoking'*, *'made you think'* and *'illuminating'*. The observation, noted above, that one of the students felt guilty after the session, was echoed by other comments that rated the parents' session as *'humbling'* and *'made me feel uneasy – because you then think about what a lot of parents are going through'*. These feelings of unease, guilt and humility all fit Brookfield's trigger event with its accompanying discomfort and perplexity. The subsequent re-appraisal of their work with parents undertaken by many of the class in subsequent sessions strongly suggests that the parents' session acted as a precipitative event or trigger for many of the students.

Period Two: 'Re-seeing' from the Parents' Perspective

Followed the parents' session with the class, a change emerged in how the students discussed their work. This was most noticeable in the fact that students began to introduce more personal anecdotes about their own interactions with parents who are service users. The discussion of service users began to move more from the general to the specific, with some students acknowledging older perceptions of parents which they now felt to be outdated and inappropriate. One student's observation on a piece of work from her early practice was typical of these discussions. *'I still get goosebumps when I think about how I treated parents in the past, I thought I knew what the mothers were going through but really I hadn't a clue.'*

This growing level of awareness of their own interactions with parents seemed to prepare the students for the introduction of the mirroring exercise which allowed students to expand and explore images of parents which they themselves were bringing to the class. Looking at the observations recorded during this second period of the research, many of them relate to students 're-seeing' themselves from the parents' point of view. The mirroring exercise also helped students develop an empathy towards parents, demonstrating an ability to imagine what parents must feel like in certain situations. This is shown in observations such as:

Occupational Therapist: I think we really have to put ourselves in [the service user's] shoes and say how would we feel if a professional came to my house or if a professional did this to me.

Psychologist: If somebody asked me that question about my child I'd be very defensive. If I was coming to that situation I need to see it from a normal parent's point of view and then see how these parents may feel to have a social worker or a psychologist coming to their house. I know I'd hate it.

In this way the mirroring exercise can be seen to have allowed students to further explore the new perspectives on parents that had been precipitated by the parents' session. The introduction of the mirroring exercise also marked a change in the pattern of class interaction. There was an observable increase in relevant intra-student debate from this session onwards; this can be seen in a decrease in both the frequency and the length of the researcher's prompts and contributions in the class transcripts. Thus the parents' session and the subsequent mirroring session can be seen to have fulfilled the criteria of an emancipatory learning experience for the students. In Cranton's (1994: 77-78) terms, exposure to the service users' experience may have been the precipitating factor for the learning, causing students to question the validity of their previously held assumptions of service users. This appears to have created Habermas's (1971: 309) hermeneutic 'communicative action', with the students re-assessing the validity of the previous meanings they have ascribed to service users. Subsequently the mirroring exercise created an environment through which alternative perspectives or meanings could be explored and considered. This fulfils the criteria for Mezirow's (1981: 14-17) learning through transformation of meaning schemes, involving reflection on assumptions and the subsequent attempts to construct new meanings for familiar situations. The intra-student discussion, which evolved around this, allowed many of the students to move into Habermas's (1984: 310) emancipatory learning domain, where self-reflection freed the students to create new meaning both for service users and for themselves in relation to those service users.

Period Three: Reflecting on Practice and Reflecting in Practice

By the final weeks of the research many of the students were able to explore and analyse aspects of their own work with service users through the case study presentations. By this stage, the students demonstrated an ability to 'stand back' from the professional/service user interactions and to reflect on the nature and quality of their work. This ability to reflect on work with service users was most frequently demonstrated in the students' references to overall changes that they had noted in their work and to changes they had noted in specific cases. In terms of overall change observations were recorded such as:

> Nurse: I've learned to value the input that parents can make, to go on supporting the subjective experiences of parents and not become concerned only with implementing change and instituting plans whilst ignoring the effects that such plans have on them.

> Psychologist: I'm becoming more vigilant in using good listening techniques – I want to assist families to seek out what they want for themselves rather than offering prescriptions from a professional.

> Nurse: I think I'm more open to listening to the parents' viewpoint, I'm more positive to their suggestions. I think that when things get tough, it's very easy to slot into Model I behaviour, particularly when you are tired or stressed. You just have to watch it, realize when it's happening and do something about it.

This description of recognizing when a professional is tending towards Model I behaviour and the reaction to this realization – *'watch it, realize what's happening and do something about it'*, is an excellent example of Schön's reflection-in-action. Reflection-in-action requires a recognition of non-productive elements in practice, adoption of new approaches and evaluation of success of new approach (Schön 1987 28-29). As Schön describes, a skilled practitioner incorporates reflection-in-action as a seamless part of practice. This is evidenced in this student's awareness of how stress or tiredness can affect her practice. Another student also demonstrated reflection-in-action in her realization that *'you have to stop yourself and think. You suddenly listen to what you are saying – you catch yourself sliding down into Model I, but once you can see what's happening you can be different'*. It is this ability to describe the intuitive understanding inherent in one's own practice which is characteristic of the reflective practitioner (Schön 1883: 276).

In this third group of recorded observations on service users, other students described changes which they had initiated in specific cases.

Nurse: The parents I've been working with, they felt they had been much more involved – they said I had really listened to them and it had helped them a lot.

Social Worker: There was a particular family I was working with and I needed to work with them to arrange respite care. It involved working with the parents, listening to them, making them part of the decision making. It wasn't me telling, it was them deciding.

Nurse: The best thing I did was I just listened to them [parents]. I recognize now that I probably say very little, but I listen. Then I reflect back to them what they have been saying from time to time so that they know I have been listening and have understood them. They have since said that it helped a lot.

All three students above are making the same important point, that listening to parents produces positive results. This realization, although outwardly simplistic, resulted from the students' ability to re-evaluate their method of interaction with the parents. Russell and Munby (1991: 165) call this 'reframing' – thinking systematically about freshly framed data, which they link to an ability to reflect-in-action. In many of the observations about parents recorded during this third period of the research, students demonstrated their capacity to 'reframe' their perspectives on parents. They also showed an awareness of how their own practice impacted on service users. As I had hoped, this allowed most of the students to fully rotate the professional/service user interaction and thus gain new and productive new perspectives on the interaction.

Time Frames for Achieving and Maintaining New Perspectives

There is a danger, in the evaluation of the structure of the research, to give the impression that all the students experienced the same level of transformative learning and reflective change and at around the same time. In reading the literature on reflective learning there is a dearth of material on the time scale in which reflective learning might be expected to occur. In simple terms, learning theorists suggest that, given the correct learning environment, most students should achieve higher levels of perspective transformation and emancipatory learning. What they fail to examine is how long students may have to be exposed to the learning environment before perspective transformation occurs.

In this research most students, both in interaction with each other and with me, achieved some level of perspective transformation – but to differing degrees and at different times, although all were exposed to the same learning environment. This research revealed that the students also achieved perspective transformation and critical learning in stages, rather than in one shift. I compared these differences to the differences in age and professional background of the students to see if any pattern emerged. In this comparison I found no connection between either age, professional background or vocal participation in group discussion and the rate at which students achieved perspective transformation and model rotation. What did emerge was the importance of offering students enough time to re-examine their attitudes to parents and to explore new parental perspectives at their own pace. Students also needed opportunities to critically appraise what such changes meant for them in their own work situation. To this end it was necessary to give time to the students in the practicum to allow them to integrate their new learning and to apply it to their own practice. The later sessions where students prepared and presented their individual case studies proved especially useful in this regard. These later sessions, which took up nine hours of the research time, appear to have offered a time of consolidation for the students during which they could explore new perspectives and then begin to incorporate them into specific case examples from their own and other's practice situations.

Following the tenets of action research, the direction of work with the class evolved in response to emerging group achievements, discoveries and needs, with my role being the introduction of reflective approaches to maximize the critical learning being achieved by the participants. Figure 8.1 demonstrates the connections between the different sessions held with the students, the phases of the reflective teaching and learning model and the three stages of parental perspectives, noted earlier in this chapter. Figure 8.1 also shows the emergence of the fifth phase of the teaching and learning model and its connection with the time span of the research in general.

Figure 8.2, presented at the conclusion of this chapter, shows how different aspects of the research can be visualized as part of the learning continuum shown in Figure 8.1.

Figure 8.1   Revised Connections between Phases of Reflective Model

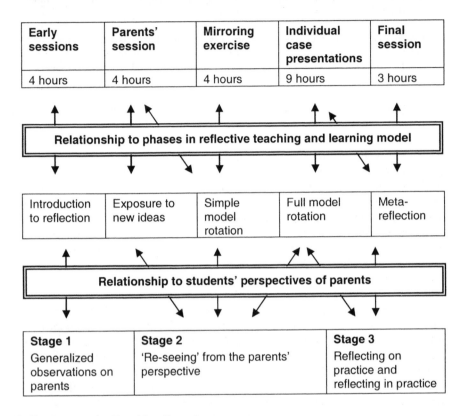

Early sessions	Parents' session	Mirroring exercise	Individual case presentations	Final session
4 hours	4 hours	4 hours	9 hours	3 hours

Relationship to phases in reflective teaching and learning model

Introduction to reflection	Exposure to new ideas	Simple model rotation	Full model rotation	Meta-reflection

Relationship to students' perspectives of parents

Stage 1	Stage 2	Stage 3
Generalized observations on parents	'Re-seeing' from the parents' perspective	Reflecting on practice and reflecting in practice

Reflections on the Teaching Experience

As discussed in the previous chapter, the last session of my work with the class had been planned as a review of our work together. During the final session the students completed a brief questionnaire on aspects of the course and changes in practice (both accomplished and potential) identified by them as a result of working with me. This questionnaire was designed both to provide evaluatory data and to help the students to focus on a wider appraisal of the course.

The initial questions on the questionnaire asked students to assess how they felt the sessions with me had affected the way they now worked with parents and families. A majority of the students reported that they considered that they now had a greater understanding of the needs of the families with whom they worked. Interestingly, in discussing this, a number of the students used terms relating to perception and viewpoint.

Nurse: I have gained insights into their [parents'] life on a day-to-day basis.
I am trying to understand their perspective [evaluation questionnaire].

Nurse: My thinking has become more reflective. I am more aware of how my approach and verbal interaction with families can really give families back some control in their lives [evaluation questionnaire].

Psychologist: I've increased my awareness of LISTENING [student's emphasis] rather than rushing in and SOLVING! I'm more aware of the importance of putting family perspectives 'on the map' in a large residential service [evaluation questionnaire].

Losing the Expert Role   This aspect of listening and not 'solving' emerged in a number of responses from students. Some students connected this increased ability to listen and to appreciate the service user's perspective to a decrease in their perception of themselves as 'having to have all the answers'. Another student commented that she was *'more ready to listen, I'm less of an expert now'*. These responses mirror what Argyris and Schön (1996: 283) describe as a reduction of defensive reasoning and an increase in productive reasoning. These students give strong indications of having moved from the position of Schön's expert (1983: 300) who is presumed to know, to the position of the reflective practitioner who is also presumed to know, but is not the only one in the situation to have relevant and important knowledge.

Implementing Reflective Practice and 'Not Going Back'   A willingness to establish a more reflective, responsive approach to parents was evident in many of the students' responses, both in earlier sessions and in the evaluatory questionnaire. It was in the final weeks of the research that students began to use the practicum as a place where they were comfortable in discussing difficulties arising from their attempts to change their approach to their work with parents. What became clear during these sessions was that, in spite of the difficulties that arose, the students were becoming increasingly convinced that they wanted to implement a reflective approach with parents. One student commented:

Nurse: Getting into that way of thinking [Model II/reflective behaviour] gets to you, once you've looked at the deeper meanings for both yourselves and the parents, how they think, how things really are for them, then you can't go back. It would probably be a whole lot easier if you could but you have to look at things differently now.

This student's reference to 'deeper meanings' seems to indicate a growing awareness of needing to look beyond the tacit attitudes that underpin professional behaviour towards parents. Her statement signals that she has undergone a real change in her perception of her relationship with parents. By doing so, she may have, in Mezirow's (1990a: 12-13) terms, undergone critical reflection and thus achieved perspective transformation. In Friere's words (1996: 77), she may have experienced 'conscientization'.

Making such a critical transformation is not achieved without difficulty. This student had also highlighted a significant factor in achieving perspective transformation or conscientization – the fact that, by reaching this state of awareness, it is very difficult, if not impossible, to return to one's previous unreflective state. By undertaking critical reflection it become difficult or impossible to 'unknow' what has been discovered; as the student had mentioned: '*You can't go back*'. What became more evident towards the end of the sessions was the number of students who were now facing previously routine work situations which, due to their abilities to fully rotate both parental and professional perspectives, had now become far less tolerable for them. A number of students used the group for support in such incidences. This is probably best exemplified in an incident discussed by Bernie, one of the psychologists. In the penultimate session of the research, Bernie discussed how a meeting with parents, which would previously have been routine practice, now presented her with considerable difficulties. The concept of 'having an answer' for service users also re-occurs in the following discussion.

> Bernie: We had a typical example last week of parents coming in for a case conference, and all the professionals concerned met half an hour before to plan the meeting, to decide what we were going to say to them. I was going to leave and say I'll come back when the parents came in. But I didn't.
>
> Doctor: But do you not have to prepare at some stage? If the professionals hadn't met up before hand, don't they have to get together?
>
> Bernie: Why? Why do the professionals have to get their side of things sorted out before they meet the parents. Why couldn't everybody involved get together at the same time. The parents should have really come in at the beginning and we could brainstorm with them, they could brainstorm with us. It's not like we had answers for them. I just feel such a coward that I didn't make a stand, refused to go in until the parents were invited in. Next time I'm doing it differently, I couldn't be part of that again, it feels so wrong now.

There is evidence in the forgoing conversation that the students are aware not only that they are now capable of seeing new and more complex parental perspectives, but that they may be working with colleagues who continue to hold the more limited, one-dimensional view of parents and their needs. For Bernie, who had fully rotated her model of these parents, she now had a new perspective on how the organization of the case conference and the behaviour of the professionals, including herself, might appear to the parents. This placed her in a dilemma of whether to work within her new, rotated model or to return to the more distant 'expert' stance of her colleagues. Her own response to the dilemma is clear: '*Next time I'm doing it differently, I couldn't be part of that again, it feels so wrong now.*' Bernie's response also confirms the earlier point of how professionals find it difficult to return to Model I behaviour once they have developed perspectives based on Model II principles.

Model II Practitioners in Model I Agency Structures

Ironically, Bernie's case highlights both the success of my teaching approach in helping the students to become reflective practitioners and a dilemma that this achievement may create. One of the nurses expressed the predicament well: '*I think that here, with you, on a Friday you can see things clearly, but you get back to work on a Monday, into the system, and the changes you want to make are much harder to implement than you thought.*' On a number of occasions students discussed the fact that the acquisition of a more reflective approach in professional practice cannot happen independently of the larger work situation. What also emerged, both before and during the final session and in the student feedback, were the difficulties inherent in adopting a more reflective approach within their own work agencies. One of the nurses described a case conference where '*we the professionals began to make authoritative statements and then the parents were looking for the "right" answers from us*'. Her new realization that neither she nor the other professionals really had 'right answers' for these parents became, for her, a source of frustration. Like the frustration noted by Bernie, this nurse also commented: '*Everybody went into Model I behaviour – I just wanted to leave, we were getting nowhere.*'

What began to emerge in the later sessions of the research was a growing awareness on the part of the students that, although their practice was becoming more reflective and taking on more Model II characteristics, many of them were working in agencies which were predominantly Model I systems. The students expressed this in different ways. In her case study Carmel had identified a Model I-type ethos in her agency in a case where she was a key worker with a family of a very young child. In this case she was not allowed to confirm or even discuss the parent's correct suspicion of autism in their daughter until a 'higher-status' professional had seen the family. This delay jeopardized the sound Model II relationship which Carmel had tried to build with the family, who then perceived that she had not shared valid information with them. One of the psychologists saw that her efforts at developing Model II practice were constrained by her agency's provision of services primarily based on the availability of funding – '*the management make decisions based on what's there, as opposed to what families really want*'. In her overall evaluation of the research, this student also commented that one of the main barriers to her becoming more reflective was her agency's tendency to marginalize service users.

A final aspect of the difficulties of working with a Model I agency structure began to emerge from a question that I asked them in the final session. Having identified with students what changes they would like to make in their work with parents, they were then posed the question 'what stops you from doing that now?' This line of enquiry has its roots in the work of Putnam (1991: 145-163) who postulated that the concept of asking such a question moves new critical learning into the reality of practice. A common theme emanated from the students' responses to this question – a feeling of powerlessness within the agency structure. Some of the students' comments described themselves as '*only a little cog in a very big wheel ... there are restrictions above me which I must acknowledge*' or '*a small fish in an agency which does not advocate a partnership model with parents*'. One of the nurses perceived her main barrier as being '*the attitudes of superiors, new ideas are usually unwelcome where I work*'. Another student described how the adoption of a pragmatic approach in a Model I agency can, at times, appear tempting to the professional. *'Sometimes it is just easier to continue doing things the way everybody else has done them, you become afraid to change things.'*

Since the issue of working in agencies with Model I values had been raised by a number of the students, I discussed with the class if they thought they risked isolating themselves within their agency by becoming more reflective in their own practice. This discussion raised the issue that, by developing more complex, reflective relationships with parents, professionals might also become more closely identified with parents. A concern was voiced that, in agencies that did not value the opinions of service users, this might also 'devalue' the reflective professional. A number of the students agreed that, although being more reflective might present difficulties in the workplace, those difficulties were outweighed by the potential benefits of reflective practice for both parents and professionals. One nurse described that as a result of working in my class, she had developed more of a *'personal honesty'* with herself and with service users and she reiterated the feeling that she would not return to a previous, unreflected position: *'I'm not prepared to go back on it, my colleagues will have to get used to it.'*

Reflective Changes

In the last session students also discussed recent pieces of work with parents with which they had been particularly pleased. One of the most interesting reports came from Annette, one of the younger nurses, who described a brief, but very well defined change into reflective practice.

Annette: I had something that was a real change in my work that I got from your class. In the unit that I work in when inquiries or one of the family rang about one of our residents we, the staff, took the call and dealt with the enquiry. Now, particularly since the Model II thinking, I will always say to the family member *'would you like to speak to your sister or brother or son'*, whatever. The first time I did it, the mother said *'why, is there something wrong?'*, but the families really like to chat with their family member now. But there was no reason why we had always taken the calls, the person with the disability was just sitting there while we took the call on their behalf, but everybody did it. We all had the conversation with family, answered questions then said to the person *'Your Mum rang'*. It was only when I, like you said, reflected on what I was doing, it really was like something out of the dark ages, you know.

Social Worker: Do a lot of the other staff still do it?

Annette: It's beginning to change since I started doing it, but it just feels so strange to me now that I ever did it. It's only a little thing, but, it's been really important to me that I made that change. You start to do things because everybody else does it that way. Then you see, reflect, on the situation from the parents' point of view and try something different just to see what will happen, and it's so different, like why didn't you see it before.

Annette's description of the small but significant change in her work practice is a good example of what Argyris and Schön (1974: 128-134) saw as the greatest achievement of participants in a practicum – devising new action strategies in their work which expose previous inconsistencies and increase effective practice.

In a subsequent discussion, Annette noted that the impetus for her to reflect-in-action came from the completion of her individual case study – *'that exercise made me think about things I "just do" at work'*. 'Just doing' is a good way to describe tacit practice that is imbedded in one-dimensional thinking. Such practice occurs primarily out of habit and professional convenience, is seldom evaluated and may be replicated, unchallenged, by successive professionals. Annette's story is evidence that the reflective teaching model had succeeded in creating an environment where some of the professionals began to examine what they 'just did' with service users and to evaluate its efficacy both for the service user and for themselves.

The Supportive Reflective Environment

A number of the students mentioned the importance of the support they received from their classmates in changing and refining their practice. Schön (1987: 38) noted that that within the practicum, the relationship between students should be as important as the relationship between student and teacher. Schön suggests that in the effective practicum students should demonstrate that they are able to adopt a coaching role with each other. It was evident in analysing the transcripts of the classes, that students in this research became increasingly comfortable in questioning and challenging each other about practice. What became most noticeable was the decrease in traditional professional boundaries, with incidences of 'higher status' professionals such as doctors and psychologists becoming open to quite probing questions on their practice from some of the nurses. This confirms Schön's (1987: 36) notion that the effective reflective practicum encourages students to stop 'thinking like a ----------'. It also adds weight to Taylor's (1997: 75-76) suggestion that, while interprofessional learning approaches remain largely *ad hoc* and unevaluated, there are indications that 'shared learning' increases a sense of professional collaboration and helps dispel interprofessional stereotyping. By focusing on shared experiences and encouraging constructive debate in the class, this group of students began to work together less as members of specific professions and more as a collaborative, cohesive group exploring new ways of working with service users.

A number of the students referred to the importance of having the support of classmates in the efforts to change their practice with parents and they also described the practicum as a 'safe' place in which to examine practice issues.

Maureen: It's good to have here [practicum] to come back to, to tease out how you're doing.

Wendy: Well I can say things here I can't say at work, kind of think out loud.

Other students used words like '*safe*' and '*familiar*' to describe the class. This was a positive finding as it supported my belief that the practicum should provide a secure environment in which to discuss practice issues, perceived failures and to re-evaluate practice. This perception of the safety of the practicum was also borne out by the number of students who chose to present case studies which related to difficulties in their work with parents and the students who asked the research group for advice with on-going practice dilemmas. The importance of the learning group and group cohesion is a major theme in adult education (Cranton 1994: 194). Boud and Walker (1998: 204) highlight the importance of constructing a learning environment which counters oppressive behaviour on the part of learners towards each other. They also stress the need to create a place of trust and respect in which reflection and exploration can flourish. If such conditions are fulfilled, and there is evidence that they were in this research, then the teacher/researcher does not retain sole responsibility for supporting students in the process of transformational learning. As Boyd (1989: 467) notes, the group can then 'provide supportive structures that facilitate an individual's work in realizing personal transformation'. An analysis of each individual's amount of participation in the class transcripts shows a diminution of the researcher's voice in later sessions, with the students more likely to explore issues and offer constructive responses to each other.

This is not to say that all students participated to the same extent in the sessions and certainly, in the analysis of class participation, some participants were more involved than others in different sessions. Cranton (1994: 154) warns that in reflective learning situations, students should never be forced into discourse. Because of this, I tried to create a variety of 'participatory options' such as written exercises and smaller group discussions to ensure that all the students remained engaged in the reflective process. As already discussed, higher levels of participation in the larger group did not show a positive correlation with the participants' ability to achieve model rotation and some of the quieter students were observed to be just as capable of rotating parental perspectives as those who were more vocal. However, the use of the written exercises and the small-group work was demonstrated as important in offering the quieter students alternative reflective environments in which they demonstrated that they were able to achieve both simple and full model rotation.

What emerged in terms of this group dynamic was that, although the students worked with parents in many different settings, they discovered a commonality in their experience of working with a particular group of service users. This commonality, combined by a growing group cohesiveness, allowed the students to explore together new ways of working with parents and to view the practicum as a safe environment in which to disclose attendant difficulties in implementing new approaches in their practice. Mezirow (1991) sees perspective transformation as having a socially interactive nature. Those making such a critically reflective step need others to test out and reinforce new perspectives – 'this can be vitally important in making transformation possible and we validate the new perspectives through rational discourse' (1991: 185). Within this research the students were observed to be increasingly at ease in hypothesizing about new perspectives in their work with parents and also increasingly able to work together to consider and discuss such perspectives. By doing so they fulfilled the criteria for what Mezirow (1991: 185) termed collective transformation.

My Own Reflections on the Teaching Experience

As noted earlier, any collaborative study has to acknowledge the importance of the role of the researcher on the progress and impartiality of the research. Schön (1991: 357) states that in reflective work there is no given, preobjectified state of affairs waiting to be uncovered through inquiry. All research findings are someone's construction of reality and, unless the researcher acknowledges her own subjective state within the research, she cannot attempt to make definite statements about her findings. Therefore, this final section will look at some of the issues which arose for me in relation to my own reflective positioning within the research. In order to help me to be rigorously reflective, this section will draw on my discussions with two critical friends which took place at different junctures throughout the course of the work, and on my own reflective journal which I kept throughout the research.

Reflecting with Critical Friends

Schön (1991: 357) demands that the reflective researcher has an obligation to become aware of her own blindness and bias in her own way of analysing the reality she has observed. My principal way of doing this was to share with two critical friends my work-in-progress throughout the research period. Both critical friends supported me by reading some of the transcripts of the sessions and then discussing pertinent issues with me. The great benefit of working with both of these critical friends has been their familiarity with both reflective theory and its application to practice, making them perceptive and challenging critics of my work. They were both very adept in their work with me – asking questions and posing conundrums that encouraged me to be more reflective in my own thinking. In my consultation sessions with the critical friends, a number of issues arose at different times around my own participation in the research.

Learning to 'Sit Around the Well'

A useful factor in the research has been the fact that I was involved in the transcription of all the video and audiotapes collected during the period. Being forced to listen to oneself, often repetitively, produces an uncomfortable awareness of weaknesses and contradictions in one's own practice. One revelation for me was the amount of talking I had done in the early sessions. Having reviewed the transcripts of an early session, one of the critical friends remarked '*you wouldn't be too good at sitting around the well*'. He was referring to Freire's reflective practitioner in developing cultures, one who waits until the co-participants have decided in which direction they wish to go. The critical friend suggested that, at the speed I have been working, I could well have re-designed an entire village community before really listening to what people have to say. A mixture of anxiety and impatience had caused me to rush the participants into what I had been tempted to see as the 'right' direction; to exercise too much control over the direction of the class. I had also expressed my own opinion too much. If the research was to be a collaborative exercise then I had to heed Taylor's (1996: 90) warning about the degree of power wielded by reflective teachers. The students had to feel that all their contribution had validity, not just those that concurred with my own opinions. When asked by one of the critical friends what I needed to do to in order to overcome the tendency to exercise too much class control, I commented:

Researcher: I've got to learn to keep my mouth shut and my ears open.

C. Friend: How will you know when you have done that?

Researcher: Em ... Perhaps when I can see that I have been able to leave a silence happen and not have rushed in and try and fill the vacuum.

C. Friend: What do you think the students would think if you left the class in silence?

Researcher: If I'm honest, I know my fear is that they might think I didn't know what to do next.

C. Friend: Model I or Model II?

Researcher: Me? Oh Model I – competent professional, all the answers.

C. Friend: So could leaving a silence be a Model II act? Leaving a space for the students to know more than you do, to say something new, to have more control in the sessions?

Researcher: Yes, it also might give the quieter ones a chance to say something. I really can't criticize them for not talking when I'm filling in all the gaps. It might also help them not to feel that I knew had a superior insight into what was right and was waiting for them to give me the right answer.

The session in which two parents came into the classroom marked an improvement in my over-participation in the sessions. Being able to sit back and watch the parents interact with the students was a considerable learning experience for me; I discovered that I did not have to 'take charge' of the class. The transcripts of the sessions from this point on show a decrease in my overall participation in discussions. It seemed that as the students grew more confident in discussing issues together, I grew more confident in letting them do so. Perhaps the reverse was also true – my increasing restraint may have allowed the students to feel more confident about comparing opinions. Whichever way it happened, the students and I began to create what Brookfield (1995: 44-45) describes as the democratic classroom where conditions are created under which all voices can be heard and in which the classroom processes are seen to open to genuine negotiation.

Assessing Success and Failure in the Class

Another aspect of my work discussed with the critical friends was the criteria I was using to measure success in the class. This followed a comment I made about one particular student as being '*very good, very bright*'. Both critical friends challenged me as to what criteria I was using to make such a judgement and asked if 'good' students were, in reality, those who agreed with my way of thinking. In my own reflective learning in this research I had begun to realize the truth of Horton's (1990: 16) words: 'if people have a strong position on something and you try and argue them into changing it, you're going to strengthen that position'. This realization became clear in how angry I had let myself become early on in the research at what I perceived as one student's unwillingness to see the necessity of reflecting on her practice. Brookfield (1995: 261) warns that resistance to critical reflection needs to be respected and understood. Cranton (1994: 107-111) notes that critical reflection and the perspective changes that it produces will be different for each individual. What I had to learn to do was to allow the students to reach their own levels of perspective change, at their own pace. Many of the students also had to question the relevance of the research in general or specific aspects of the classes before they could continue in their rotation of their perspectives. Mezirow (1990b: 364) notes that disequilibrium is a necessary part of the transformative learning process and that learners will become engaged in critical evaluation of the reflective 'system' as they seek for new perspectives. Initially I tended to react defensively to such actual and implied criticism. Finding this response frustrating for both the students and myself, I attempted increasingly to incorporate such criticisms into group discussions. I too had to learn to rotate my perspective of the students – from expecting them to be co-operative with me, to appreciating new and important ideas that they had to impart to the class. Also as the group became more cohesive, there was a growing sense of co-operative 'ownership' of the research process, so responding to criticism became more of a group function than an individual student/researcher dialogue.

My Own Learning Journey

What became clearer to me, having been able to analyse and evaluate transcripts of all the sessions, was that during the research, I experienced a very similar reflective learning 'journey' to many of the students. Like them, I had to learn to listen more and not to rush and try and solve matters. I too had to discover that I did not have all the answers nor did I always have to be an expert. In fact, the more expert I appeared, the less opportunity I gave the students to explore their own experiences and to find learning in such an exploration. Brookfield (1995: 255) indicates that the main factor likely to encourage reflective behaviour is having it modelled by senior practitioners or teachers. In retrospect there were times, particularly at the beginning of the research, when I encouraged students to look for Model II aspects in their own practice, while I was maintaining a Model I-type, non-reflective control over the class. Asked by both critical friends why I tended towards this behaviour, I had to admit to a mixture of anxiety and fear. I commented, in a session with one critical friend, that '*I had an overall plan and fear kept me from letting that plan go.*' In a way I had to 'let go' of my research plan as if it were a fixed pre-determined schema, before I could let the research become emancipatory. Doing this generated a confidence that came from a number of sources including my growing respect for the students and their abilities. I had also begun to acknowledge a self-serving rationale for adopting a Model II approach. With the critical friends' help, I realized that the less I tried to control the direction in which the class was going, the more useful was the data I was able to gather. This had a strong parallel with what the students were discovering – that imposing less control on service users often resulted in the development of a more productive relationship with them.

Becoming Self-reflective

What has been most interesting for me in this research is the realization of how easily I could see the rationale for a Model II, reflective approach in the students' work, yet how long it took me to recognize the need for reflection-in-action in my own work. Even at the end of the research sessions, when I thought that I had reached a high level of self-awareness, analysis of the transcripts still showed my tendency to revert to an expert position. This may be related to a difficulty I have observed in my reconciling the joint roles as researcher and teacher with the class. One of the critical friends helped me see that I might have a much stronger sense of myself as a teacher than as a researcher, and that, in tense situations, I tended to revert to a Model I 'teaching mode'.

C. Friend: Have you ever worked out which is the 'real' you in the class? Do you feel like you are really a researcher or really a teacher?

Researcher: I know which role I'm much more comfortable with, being a teacher. I know I'm a good teacher but I'm not so sure I'm a good researcher.

C. Friend: So, when things get tricky in the class, when you feel pressurized, what do you feel like doing?

Researcher: Then the teaching role feels much safer and I know I have to fight the tendency to give them some information – give them the right answers. The teaching role feels more protective – in a selfish way, for me, not for the students. I feel more protected as a Model I teacher than a Model II critical researcher.

This realization shows how older, Model I behaviour can be so alluring, especially in times of stress. It also helped me to appreciate how difficult it must have been for some of the students to achieve perspective transformation and how much risk they had taken in applying the new perspectives in often hostile agency environments where they were 'expected' to act in a particular Model I manner.

If this research is to be persuasive and the ideas transferable, then the research has had to be described in as transparent a way as possible. In an action research project such as this the researcher cannot be removed from the research.

Therefore it was necessary for me to show personal honesty in the writing-up of the research. My use of critical friends proved essential to the maintenance of that honesty. Their contribution ensured that my own reflective journey was repeatedly double-loop tested. Lewin (1946: 153) spoke about the necessity for honesty and fair-mindedness in action research 'the scientist has to look facts straight in the face, even when they do not agree with his prejudices'. By doing this I have realized that moving towards reflective practice is far from an easy shift in perspective. Instead, it is a continuing struggle against older, entrenched, defensive responses and behaviours that exist at the very roots of the notion of expertise and professionalism. Achieving change does not happen without an honest acknowledgement of these defensive behaviours. It also includes a willingness to surrender those attitudes which, although ultimately non-productive, appear to reinforce us as competent professionals. Becoming reflective professionals causes us to acknowledge that, in Brookfield's (1995: 257) words, we 'are visibly evolving as learners, always in the process of formation'. As I have learned in this research, this acknowledgement is not achieved without a degree of perceived risk to our professional identity and a large amount of personal honesty.

Summary

This chapter has outlined the overall trends which emerged in the research as a whole. It has also included evaluation by the research participants and the personal reflections of the researcher. It was noted in a discussion of the structure of the research, that certain sections of the researcher's reflective model were associated with specific developments in the reflective learning of the participating students. This part of the research ends with a diagrammatic representation of the phases of the reflective teaching and learning model matched to the issues and changes charted in this chapter. Figure 8.2 documents these changes, including the students' ability to rotate parental perspectives, their references to the typology of parents, and the impact of the agency structure and ethos on the students' ability to become more reflective in their work with families. It also notes both the changes in the students' work with parents which transpired during the course of the research and the changes noted by the researcher in her own practice during this period. Setting out these changes in diagrammatic form presents a cohesive picture of a number of interconnected issues in the course of the research. It also attempts to display how increases and decreases in certain behaviours occurred at different times over the course of the research.

It is the nature of action research that its results, such as those discussed in this chapter and the observed changes shown in Figure 8.2, remain subtle transformations in what is predominantly a social process between the researcher and the researched. One of the things which makes action research 'research' is that it aims at the systematic development of knowledge in a self-critical community of practitioners (Carr and Kemmis 1986: 188). The results reported in this chapter represent a deliberate process of emancipation for both the researcher and the researched from the often-unseen constraints of habit, assumption, custom and precedent. They present a case of listening acutely, to hear silences and ellipses, as well as what is evident; of seeking to draw others and oneself into discursive dissonance in order to find that which can be agreed as the basis for that which will be done that no-one can deny the wisdom of doing (Clegg 1994: 171).

Figure 8.2 Connection between Phases of Model

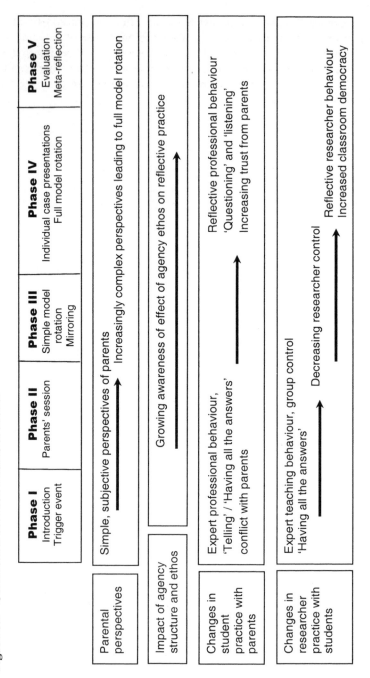

Chapter 9

Final Thoughts

The Completed Reflective Teaching and Learning Model

By its nature, professional practice contains tacit and habitual aspects that ultimately can limit the professional's ability to respond appropriately and effectively to client need. This reflective teaching and learning model has been designed to find, acknowledge and challenge these routine and predictable aspects of professional practice and to generate approaches to service users which are more responsive and effective. By utilizing the principles of reflective teaching and critical learning, the model has been designed to encourage professionals to explore significant aspects of their current practice, to attempt new, more considered methods of working with their service users and subsequently to analyse the effectiveness of such new approaches. Central to the model is the importance of creating a teaching and learning environment that encourages and challenges professionals to confront their perceptions of the service users with whom they work and to examine how such perceptions influence their practice.

The completed model (shown in Figure 9.1) consists of five phases with each phase relating to the five action research phases undertaken in this research. The symbolism of the diagram reflects the changes experienced by the students as they moved through the phases of the model. The first phase of the model relates to the routine, generalized perspectives of service users that would expected to be found at the start of working with a professional group. This phase is symbolized in Figure 9.1 by the use of a square, upright box, indicative of the fixed, 'hard-line' linear perspectives likely to be found at this point in the model. Specific exercises used in this phase of the model are simple, reflective exercises, either in verbal small-group format or in written form. These short exercises also work as icebreakers, preparing students for the discursive, non-didactic style used in the model and helping them to become more familiar with working together as a group in the practicum.

These exercises lead to the first perspective shift – precipitated by an exposure to client perspectives, particularly as articulated by service users themselves. This exposure is supported by continuing reflective exercises and group discussion which encourage the professionals to evaluate their responses to the service users in the practicum. In Figure 9.1 this phase is symbolized by a rotated square, indicative of the 'tilting of perspective' inherent in this phase. This initial movement, which occurs for participants in this phase, allows them to begin to move from fixed, habitual client perspectives to newer, more open ideas about those with whom they work.

The third phase of the teaching and learning model is characterized by the introduction of simple model rotation exercises. By use of reflective activities, the professionals are encouraged and challenged to 're-see themselves' from the client's perspective. The most significant exercise used in this phase is the 'mirroring' exercise. Professionals are also encouraged to expand and explore the new client perspectives that they are developing. This phase is symbolized in Figure 9.1 by a more rounded, softer shape denoting the 'softer', more considered attitudes which participants should be able to display towards their service users at this phase in the model. Success in this third phase also indicates that the professional is ready to move on to full model rotation.

Full model rotation involves more complex teaching and coaching approaches that encourage professionals to examine the assumptions underlying their thoughts and actions. Reflective approaches in this phase involve activities such as case study presentations, client plans, critical questioning, and reflective analytical devices such as the 4.Q.C.A. These are designed to help professionals not only to see new aspects of the service users, but also to consider new ways of thinking and acting with those service users. Full model rotation appears, in Figure 9.1, as a turning circle which is symbolic of the ability of the participants in this phase to reflectively turn and explore new perspectives not only of the client model but also to explore their own role with the professional/client interaction. This fourth phase of the teaching and learning model evolves into the fifth and final phase, where these new, fully rotated perspectives are translated into new practice approaches attempted by the professionals which are then explored and analysed within the practicum.

An important aspect of this final phase is the existence within the practicum of a supportive milieu where professionals can discuss the challenges and outcomes of their new approaches. Fear of failure is a significant barrier to both individual and group change. This research has demonstrated that it is possible to create a learning environment where professionals can move beyond the fear of not being a 'successful' professional and to consider uncertainty and risk-taking in new practice approaches as productive and auspicious. This research has shown that by the final phases of the teaching and learning model, it is possible to have generated enough trust within the practicum to support and encourage professionals to attempt new and potentially uncertain ways of working. These new approaches involve professionals taking the risk of dropping a professional 'façade' and beginning to work more transparently and collaboratively with service users. The final phase is symbolized by an ever-changing, interactive circle where professionals can explore and evaluate new ways of appreciating and working with service users in a supportive, yet challenging environment.

Figure 9.1 Completed Reflective Teaching and Learning Model

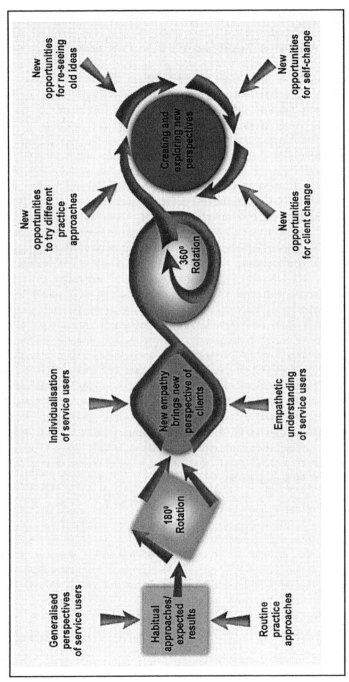

Features of the Reflective Teaching and Learning Model

A Multi-phased Approach to Reflective Teaching and Learning

As discussed above, this model has five distinct phases, each phase characterized by different reflective teaching approaches and each phase is designed to encourage and support different levels of reflective learning. This approach represents a development in reflective teaching and learning. Other research (Britzman 1991; Erickson and MacKinnon 1991; Brookfield and Preskill 1999) has noted the importance of reflective teaching approaches and has monitored students' learning gains in such environments. By partializing the reflective teaching experience and by designing new teaching approaches most appropriate to each phase the learning achievements expected of students at each phase of the model are made clearly explicit. Through the use of this reflective teaching model, it is now possible to appreciate distinct learning phases undertaken by students and to appreciate the most effective way to support their future development into more complex reflective learning. By partialising the teaching and learning experience in this way, this teaching model is responsive to individual differences in the students' progress with their reflective learning, so that more subtle changes can be noted and fostered.

A unique feature of the model is the inclusion, in each phase, of specific teaching approaches that appreciate and are geared towards different levels of reflective learning experienced by the students in the developing practicum. These include the Eco-map and professional cliché exercises used in the early stages, the mirroring exercise developed for simple model rotation and the more complex case study presentation, augmented by the 4.Q.C.A., which encourages full model rotation. It is important to note that the phases of the teaching and learning model have not been developed as a series of technical exercises that merely require replication. Instead, they represent a framework within which a reflective teacher and his/her students can begin to examine together some critical new ways of thinking about how they work.

Role of the Reflective Teacher

The success of a teaching model of this nature depends on the willingness of a reflective teacher to enter the learning experience in collaboration with students. By doing so reflective teachers are able to examine and change their own practice in the same way as they expect the professional students to examine and change their practice. In this way reflective teachers cannot escape also becoming reflective researchers, constantly monitoring not only what is happening to the professionals being taught, but also monitoring their own reactions and responses in the process.

One of the benefits of this type of planned reflective teaching is that it allows the teacher/researcher and the professionals/students to embark on a reflective journey together which will, each time, have a unique outcome. Each outcome, however, adds to the collective understanding of what it means to be a professional and also what it means to be a teacher. The value of the five phases within this model is that they offer a framework within which the teacher and students can develop an increasing appreciation of their perceptions on practice. The specific phases of the framework are designed to allow the students and teacher to embark on a reflective journey with the support of definite guidelines which help chart their progress towards increasingly reflective practice. This framework allows students to become more reflective in a gradual manner, building upon early small changes in their practice. It also allows individual students to accomplish different phases of the teaching and learning model at various times. The differentiation between phases – such as generalized client perspectives, simple model rotation and full model rotation, as demonstrated in this teaching and learning model – also gives the teacher/researcher specific milestones against which to measure the progress of individual students. Thus, some students, who may not be working at the same pace as others, can develop reflective capabilities in their own way.

Lastly, the phases of the model also allow for the teacher/researcher to judge the overall accomplishments of each student at the end of the practicum. Rather than viewing the ability to become more reflective as an amorphous and somewhat mysterious personal transition, the model allows for the individual progress of each student to be appreciated. While some students may, even before they enter the practicum, be intrinsically reflective individuals, others may have to undertake significant personal challenges to accomplish simple model rotation. Seeing reflection as a series of interconnected phases allows each individual to reach his or her own reflective potential within a supportive framework.

Service Users in the Reflective Process

One of the most significant findings in this research has been the importance of the contribution of two service users on the class of professional students and on the researcher herself. The analysis of students' observations recorded shortly after their session with the parents revealed significant changes in the students' overall comments and observations on parents. Instead of the generalized opinions on parents recorded in the first session, students began to adopt a more individualized view of parents and to talk more about their own work with specific families. As has already been discussed, the parents' session provided a trigger or precipitating event for the students that enabled many of the professionals to begin the process of critical learning and perspective transformation. The design of the teaching model also ensured that this exposure to service users' viewpoints was supported by specific reflective teaching approaches, which helped the students to integrate that experience into the wider reflective model. The introduction of the 'mirroring exercise' and the implementation of simple model rotation immediately after this precipitative event maximized the impact that the parents' session had had on the students.

Theoreticians and researchers in the area of reflective practice have, traditionally, attempted to encourage critical learning and perspective transformation with different individuals and groups by working with them in ways which help them explore their interactions with others. Schön worked in this way with professionals in the area of psychotherapy, engineering, musicology, teaching and architecture. Schön and other researchers (Schön and Bamberger 1991: 186-209; Newberg 1991: 65-83) attempted to help practitioners to appreciate the voice of the client in their practice. However their work with practitioners remained with the professionals alone and did not incorporate their service users – the patients, pupils or consumers of the professional service – as part of the reflective turn. Offering professionals the opportunity to hear, at first hand, the reality of what it is like to be a recipient of their service is a powerful learning experience for service users and professionals alike. As demonstrated in this research, it was also an important learning experience for the reflective teacher. In particular, the inclusion of parents into the research structure permitted me to develop a less directive stance with the students. Instead of feeling obliged to 'defend' and 'teach about' the client's position, the parent's participation allowed me to 'stand back' and observe the interaction between students and client, with an accompanying observable lessening in my didactic approaches with the class.

Exposure to the service users' perspective should not be considered a way of 'shaming' or embarrassing professionals into change. For example, a number of the students in this research expressed initial feelings of guilt and humility having listened to the parents' personal experiences. Helping professionals confront old practice habits and explore newer, more considered approaches does not work merely by making professionals feel badly about how they have behaved in the past. Instead what is needed is an ongoing reflective learning environment where they can go beyond such initial responses, learning how they can now incorporate and develop the client's perspectives into their perception of their own professionalism. The initial discomfort of perplexity generated by the client's evidence can then be developed into a longer, more profound process of reflection and change.

The client's experience can, therefore, be seen to be central to the learning process. However, it must also be both preceded and followed by reflective learning approaches which help students both prepare for, and subsequently synthesize, their reactions to the client's perspective. Some professional educational programmes invite speakers from client/service users groups as 'guest speakers' to talk about their experiences, but most of these remain isolated incidences, relatively unconnected to the overall learning schema of the students. What this research demonstrates is the importance of fully incorporating the client perspective within such a teaching and learning scheme and following up such an exposure to the client's point of view with learning techniques designed to develop and maximize the perspective change that has been precipitated.

Application of the Reflective Model to Professional Training in Different Settings

This book has concentrated on the application of a reflective teaching model in a specific context – that of professionals in relation to their work with parents who have a child with an intellectual disability. The model may also offer a framework within which any group of professionals can be enabled to explore their perceptions of the service users with whom they work. The initial phases allow professionals to become accustomed to a reflective environment and to move away from the idea of 'expert' professionals providing 'expert' answers. Exposure to service users' experiences in the practicum allow for the first changes in perspective rotation, backed up by increasingly complex reflective teaching and learning techniques. As the group begins to test out alternative ways of thinking and acting, the practicum then becomes a practice laboratory, where such new approaches are explored and evaluated. Finally professionals can assess the implications of their full-time return to the workplace, having had the opportunity to consider some fundamental changes in the way they work.

Previous research has tended to focus on fostering more reflective approaches in single professional groups (Newberg 1991; Gleed 1996; Quinn 1999) or on professionals working within specific agencies (Forester 1991; Argyris and Schön 1996). This research has demonstrated that the new teaching model can be used with a group of professionals from different professional backgrounds working in different style agencies and from a wide geographical area. The commonality between participants in this research was their shared interest in working more effectively with a particular group of service users. This focused the reflective teaching and learning around the issue of client interaction rather than around a work setting or around the overall professional training of one specific professional group. All the health and social service professionals participating in this research – nurses, doctors, social workers, occupational therapists, teachers and psychologists – would be termed 'person professionals' (Goode 1969: 297-304). Taylor (1997: 4), in her work on professional education, considered that there were common interests and dilemmas in the development of new learning styles which transcended professional boundaries, particularly in 'interpersonal professionals' – those whose work occurs primarily through face-to-face interactions with service users (Ellis 1992: 69). This research has developed and tested a model that is capable of engendering new reflective learning in the area of profession/service user interaction for any group of 'person' or 'interpersonal' professionals. The shape of the new model, including the specific reflective teaching approaches in each of its phases, is broad enough to allow it to be used in professional training and development in any group of professionals whose work brings them into face-to-face contact with their service users.

Boud and Knights (1996: 32) recommend the introduction of learning activities into health and social service programmes that promote different types and degrees of reflection. They caution, however, that effective new reflective teaching approaches need to be substantiated by research into the nature of reflection and into the efficacy of specific reflective teaching methods. Ixer (1999: 520-522) warns that the inclusion of reflection as an assessed competence in professional social work education may be potentially oppressive towards students. However, this presupposes that reflection is perceived as a competence which can or should be measured in this way. Reflection, by its nature is a personal, idiosyncratic act performed in a unique way and within a unique framework by each individual. The idea of requiring students to demonstrate an ability to reflect as a mandatory part of professional training places the whole nature of reflection itself in jeopardy. As Boud (1999: 123) notes, assessment is about the presentation of the student's abilities and expertise. Reflection, however, is about a lack of certainty and the presence of discrepancy – 'there is a danger that assessment will obliterate the very practices of reflection ... the assessment procedure celebrates certainty while reflection thrives on doubt'. The objective of this reflective teaching model has not been to 'teach' students how to reflect, but to create a milieu where, if they chose to, reflection could occur. To turn reflection into a necessary, assessed competency is to devalue its nature and to reduce it to a Model I technical competency, rather that an integral and voluntary component of Model II practices.

In terms of professional training and education, reflective teaching and learning cannot be regarded as an extra 'subject' to be included in a curriculum. Instead, it needs to be seen as part of an overall rationale for the design and delivery of professional education (Boud 1999: 122). Within professional training for health and social service professionals, creative new courses have been developed (Taylor 1997; Taylor et al 1999; Burgess et al 1999) which incorporate such an overall reflective structure and which also include such aspects as self-assessment and portfolio presentation. My reflective teaching and learning model is designed to fit into such an overall reflective context. The reflective teaching approaches in its component phases complement other reflective approaches used in professional reflective education such as critical incident analysis, learning journals and the use of peer learning support.

Permitted Uncertainty and the Nature of Professionalism

This teaching model has aimed at providing a supportive structure that encourages experimentation, exploration and evaluation, all of which are central to personal and professional transformation. However professionalism, by its nature, tends to stress the importance of irrefutable, expert knowledge. The idea that it may be helpful for the developing professional to admit to and to learn from the difficulties, anomalies and dilemmas inherent in their professional practice runs contrary to many of the principles of professionalism. Therefore the creation of an environment which emancipates professionals from the obligation of always having to be right is a difficult but necessary part of encouraging personal reflection, critical learning and professional development.

This new teaching model has been designed to initiate and support such a learning environment. The research revealed that a significant learning step taken by many of the student participants was the realization that they did not have to have all the answers for their service users. This was supported by their recognition that, unless they asked questions and received answers from service users, they were limited in the progress they could make with those service users. They further realized that, by being able to lose the mantle of unconditional expert, they were also better placed to discover and profit from the knowledge and abilities of their service users.

Creating such an environment of permitted uncertainty within a university environment, which by its nature is associated with academic expertise and certainty, is potentially contradictory. There is an assumption that any university-based teaching will involve a transfer of knowledge from an 'expert' teacher to an untutored student. As revealed in this research some students found the lack of didactic teaching in my approach initially disquieting and I noted the importance of having an introductory phase in the teaching and learning model in order to address this issue. Having done so, the design of the teaching and learning model allowed students to explore their practice experiences at a level that encouraged them to question their fundamental ideas and attitudes towards service users. This questioning and the change in practice that it engendered drew from the new knowledge that the students were gaining about themselves. Thus the reflective teacher was not giving answers to the students, but was creating a milieu where students, both individually and collectively, were finding new answers for themselves. This is not to say that a reflective teacher does not encourage and facilitate students to acquire new information and knowledge, but he/she does so in a way which allows them to assess the value and suitability of such knowledge for their own practice.

The success of realizing that, in their professional work, students do not necessarily have to hold all the answers for their service users, may well depend on how well a reflective teacher can also model permitted uncertainty. In my application of this teaching model in a university setting I was attempting to use a Model II reflective teaching approach in a predominantly Model I teaching environment. Somewhat reluctantly at times, I realized that my own role in the reflective teaching model had to avoid the provision of expert answers for the students. I also learned that, as a reflective teacher, I could encourage critical self-reflection by being open about my own practice dilemmas, thus mirroring some of the issues that the professional students were facing in their attempts to be less expert in their own practice.

The Benefits of Reflective Practice

An important point arising from the students' evaluation of the research was the indication that their growing ability to practice in a more reflective way had benefits not just for service users but also for the professionals themselves. Students reported a general increase in the quality of relationships that they were now able to make with parents and they saw that the parents seemed able to discuss issues of a more complex and personal nature with them as a result of their adoption of a more reflective approach with them. They also perceived that 'better' end results could be achieved with service users when reflective approaches were utilized as they reduced the occurrences of win/lose situations and increased the likelihood of consensus-led outcomes between professionals and service users.

Reflective practice cannot merely be about developing more complex perspectives on service users. To be effective in the long run, it also has to offer something tangible to the professional. In simple terms, if Model II reflective practice is to endure, then it has to make life easier for the professionals as well as for those with whom they work. This should occur because, by becoming more aware of the client's real needs, the reflective practitioner should provide a more accurate, appropriate and ultimately more productive response to that client. If this benefit to the professional does not occur, then the rationale for the professional to continue to develop a reflective ethos in the long term will be considerably undermined.

Last Thoughts

Professionals have become essential to the functioning of society. They make and enforce laws, control commercial and technical enterprise, provide education and take care of those who are sick, disabled or needy. Individuals, in different ways, are dependent upon professionals and, because of this, professionals are valued and revered to varying degrees by society as a whole. Above all, to those service users who require their services, professionals are powerful people. The danger, inherent in such power, is that professionals can begin to believe that they have easy, transferable answers to the unique problems posed by service users. When this occurs, the service user's needs become secondary to a demonstration of professional expertise and the experience and capabilities which service users bring to a professional encounter can be ignored. At best, this makes it less likely that the professional solution offered to the client is the one that is the most appropriate. At worst, service users experience frustration, disappointment and, ultimately, disillusionment with professionals' abilities to respond appropriately to their needs.

Good reflective teaching should beget better reflective practice, not only for the professionals being taught, but also for the teacher himself or herself. John Dewey (1916: 188) said that 'the educator's part in the enterprise of education is to furnish an environment which stimulates responses and directs the learner's outcome'. Through this research I have attempted to establish that the provision of a creative, stimulating and reflective environment can provide both learner and teacher with the means to grow in understanding and awareness not just of themselves, but also of those with whom they work. The reflective model developed in this research offers both teachers and professionals the opportunity to review and restructure their work in a way that can make it more accessible to those they aim to serve. It also offers teachers, professionals and those with whom they work a relationship which is more considered, more responsive and, ultimately more likely to achieve long-lasting and meaningful change.

> To cultivate unreflective external activity is to foster enslavement, for it leaves the person at the mercy of appetite, sense and circumstance (Dewey 1933: 67).

Appendix A

Guidelines for Completing Agency System Eco-map

This exercise allows students to examine the structure of the agency in which they work using diagrammatic representation. It should help students to gain greater insight into the overall management structure of the agency, the patterns of internal communication, and to suggest changes to facilitate greater involvement and equity for staff and service users.

The agency map should show the agency from the student's own point of view and the representation begins from that point. Students are free to be inventive in the way they wish to set out their map and the symbols shown on the next page are offered as a guide. The main map should be drawn on A3 size paper and students are encouraged to use colour to help them in preparing their work. Artistic ability is not required for this exercise!

Try and locate 'systems' in your map – groups which have a distinct identity from your perspective. These systems can be encircled on the map in colour. If the agency is large and students have difficulty in keeping all their work on one page, they may choose to make a separate 'mini-map' for examination of a particular area of the agency, especially if the relationships within that section are significant.

Please remember to include service users and their families in your map.

Reflection in Action

Eco-map Symbols

Symbols used in this agency eco-map are drawn from systemic family therapy (McGoldrick and Gerson 1985: 9-45)

Male: ▢

Female: ◯

Strong Relationship/good communication:
(Very close relationships can be
represented by double lines)

Tenuous/Weak Relationship,
Poor Communication:

Stressful Relationship:

Conflictual Relationships:

Flow of Energy or Resources:

One-way Communication:

Appendix B

Case Study Presentation

How to Record the Process

1. Identify an important problem/issue which you have tried to solve with a service user. There are no limits to the subject selected, except that you should see the interaction as having been important to your work.

2. Describe the steps you took in order to resolve the problem. With whom did you meet? What was the purpose of the meeting as you recall it? Identify one specific meeting with the service user/s which you feel was particularly important or significant.

3. Divide the next few pages in half. In the right-hand column, write the conversation which occurred between you and the service user/s, as you best remember it. Choose the part of the conversation or interview which you feel was significant for you. Begin with what you said, then what the other(s) said, then what you said, and so on for about three pages. You can write more if you want to.

In the left-hand column write any thoughts and feelings you had as the conversation proceeded. Be as honest as you can in recording your own thoughts and feelings. The object of this exercise is not to present a 'perfect' case, but to analyse what happens in interactions with service users and to reflect on our own reactions to situation such as confrontation, distress or argument.

Bibliography

Argyris, C. (1957) *Personality and Organization: The Conflict between System and the Individual*, New York, London, Harper and Row.

Argyris, C. (1960) *Understanding Organizational Behaviour*, Illinois, Dorsey Press.

Argyris, C. (1962) *Interpersonal Competence and Organisational Effectiveness*, Illinois, Irwin.

Argyris, C. (1964) *Integrating the Individual and the Organization*, New York, Wiley.

Argyris, C. (1965) *Organization and Innovation*, Homewood, Illinois, Richard D. Irwin.

Argyris, C. (1982) *Reasoning, Learning and Action: Individual and Organizational*, San Francisco, Jossey-Bass.

Argyris, C. (1994) 'Good Communication that Blocks Learning', *Harvard Business Review*, Vol. 72, No. 4: 77-85.

Argyris, C., Putnam, R. and McLain Smith, D. (1985) *Action Science: Concepts, Methods, and Skills for Research and Intervention*, San Francisco, Jossey-Bass.

Argyris, C. and Schön, D.A. (1974) *Theory in Practice: Increasing Personal Effectiveness*. San Francisco, Jossey-Bass.

Argyris, C. and Schön, D.A. (1978) *Organizational Learning*, Reading, Massachusetts, Addison-Wesley Publishing Company.

Argyris, C. and Schön, D.A. (1992) 'Introduction to the Classic Paperback', a new introductory section (xi-xxvi) to C. Argyris and D.A. Schön (1974) *Theory in Practice: Increasing Personal Effectiveness*, San Francisco, Jossey-Bass.

Argyris, C. and Schön, D.A. (1996) *Organizational Learning II*, Massachusetts, Addison-Wesley Publishing Company.

Ashby, W.R. (1960) *Design for a Brain*, New York, John Wiley and Sons.

Axtelle and Burnett (1970) 'Dewey on Education and Schooling', in J.A. Boydston (ed.), *Guide to the Works of John Dewey*, Carbondale Ill, Southern Illinois University Press.

Bamberger, J. and Schön, D.A. (1991) 'Learning as Reflective Conversation with Materials', in Frederick Steier (ed.), *Research and Reflexivity*, London, Sage Publications.

Bannister, D. and Fransella, F. (1971) *Inquiring Man: The Theory of Personal Constructs*, Harmonsworth, Penguin.

Basseches, M. (1984) *Dialectical Thinking and Adult Development*, Norwood, N.J. Ablex.

Bawden, R. (1991) 'Towards Action Research Systems', in O. Zuber-Skerritt (ed.), *Action Research for Change and Development*, Aldershot, Avebury.

Berman, M. (1981) *The Re-Enchantment of the World*, Ithaca and London, Cornell University Press.

Bernstein, R.J. (ed.) (1985) *Habermas and Modernity*, Oxford, Blackwell.

Bernstein, R.J. (1991) *The New Constellation: The Ethical-Political Horizons of Modernity/Postmodernity*, Cambridge, MIT Press.

Bolan, R.S. (1980) 'The Practitioner as Theorist: The Phenomenology of the Professional Episode', *Journal of the American Planning Association*, Vol. 46, No. 3, July: 261-273.

Boud, D. (1999) 'Avoiding the Traps: Seeking Good Practice in the Use of Self-Assessment and Reflection in Professional Courses', *Social Work Education*, Vol. 18, No. 2, June: 121-132.

Boud, D. and Walker, D. (1998) 'Promoting Reflection in Professionals Courses: The Challenge of Context', *Studies in Higher Education*, Vol. 23, No. 2: 191-206.

Boud, D., Keogh, R. and Walker, D. (eds) (1985) *Reflection: Turning Experience into Learning*, London, Kogan Page.

Boud, D. and Knights, S. (1996) 'Course Design for Reflective Practice', in N. Gould and I. Taylor (eds), *Reflective Learning for Social Work*, Aldershot, Arena.

Boyd, R.D. (1989) 'Facilitating Personal Transformation in Small Groups', *Small Group Behaviour*, Vol. 20, No. 4: 459-474.

Britzman, D. (1991) *Practice Makes Practice: A Critical Study of Learning to Teach*, Albany, State University of New York Press.

Brookfield, S. (1987) *Developing Critical Thinkers: Challenging Adults to Explore Ways of Thinking and Acting*, San Francisco, Jossey-Bass.

Brookfield, S. (1990) *The Skilful Teacher: On Technique, Trust and Responsiveness in the Classroom*, San Francisco, Jossey-Bass.

Brookfield, S. (1993) 'Self Directed Learning', *Adult Educational Quarterly*, Vol. 43, No. 4: 227-242.

Brookfield, S. (1995) *Becoming a Critically Reflective Teacher*, San Francisco, Jossey-Bass.

Brookfield, S. and Preskill, S. (1999) *Discussion as a Way of Teaching: Tools and Techniques for University Teachers*, Buckingham UK, The Society for Research into Higher Education and Open University Press.

Burgess, H., Baldwin, M., Dalrymple, J. and Thomas, J. (1999) 'Developing Self-Assessment in Social Work Education', *Social Work Education*, Vol. 18, No. 2, June: 133-146.

Burnard, P. (1995a) 'Nurse Educators' Perceptions of Reflection and Reflective Practice: A Report of a Descriptive Study', *Journal of Advanced Nursing*, Vol. 21: 1167-1174.

Burnard, P. (1995b) *Learning Human Skills: An Experiential And Reflective Guide for Nurses*, 3rd ed., Oxford, Butterworth-Heinemann.

Candy, P.C. (1990) 'Constructivism and the Study of Self-Direction in Adult Learning', *Studies in the Education of Adults*, 21: 95-116.

Carr, W. and Kemmis, S. (1983) *Becoming Critical: Knowing Through Action Research*, Victoria, Deakin University.

Carr, W. and Kemmis, S. (1986) *Becoming Critical: Education, Knowledge and Action Research*, Victoria, Deakin University.

Clegg, S. (1994) 'Research Training at Leeds Metropolitan University', *The Journal of Graduate Education*, Vol. 1, Issue 2.

Cohen, B. (1985) 'Skills, Professional Education and the Disabling University', *Studies in Higher Education*, Vol. 10, No. 2: 175-186.

Cranton, P. (1994) *Understanding and Promoting Transformative Learning – A Guide for Educators of Adults*, San Francisco, Jossey-Bass.

Dale, N. (1996) *Working with Families of Children with Special Needs – Partnership and Practice*, London, Routledge.

DeLong, J. (1996) 'Facilitating and Supporting Action Research by Teachers and Principals: Self-Study of a Superintendent's Role', unpublished paper given at conference on *Self-Study in Teacher Education: Empowering our Future* Herstmonceux Castle, East Sussex, England August 5-8, 1996.

Deshler, D. (1990) 'Conceptual Mapping: Drawing Charts of the Mind', in J. Mezirow and Associates, *Fostering Critical Reflection in Adulthood, A Guide to Transformative and Emancipatory Learning*, San Francisco, Jossey-Bass.

Dewey, J. (1902) *The Child and The Curriculum*, Chicago, University of Chicago Press.

Dewey, J. (1916) *Democracy and Education*, New York, The Free Press.

Dewey, J. (1933) *How We Think*, New York, Heath.

Dewey, J. (1974) *John Dewey on Education: Selected Writings* [R.D. Archambault, ed.] Chicago, University of Chicago Press.

Dominelli, L. (1998) 'Anti-Oppressive Practice in Context', in Adams, R., Dominelli, L. and Payne, M., *Social Work – Themes, Issues and Critical Debates*, Basingstoke, Macmillan.

Elden, M. and Chisholm, R.F. (1993) 'Emerging Varieties of Action Research: Introduction to the Special Issue', *Human Relations*, Vol. 46, No. 2: 121-142.

Ellis, R. (1992) 'An Action-Focus Curriculum for the Interpersonal Professions', in R. Barnett (ed.), *Learning to Effect*, Buckingham, The Society for Research into Higher Education and Open University Press.

Eraut, M. (1995) 'Schön Shock', *Teachers and Teaching: Theory and Practice*, Vol. 1: 9-22.

Erickson, G.L. and MacKinnon, A.M. (1991) 'Seeing Classrooms in New Ways: On Becoming a Science Teacher', in D.A. Schön (ed.), *The Reflective Turn: Case Studies In and On Educational Practice*, New York, Teachers College, Columbia University.

Etzioni, A. (ed.) (1969) *The Semi-Professions and their Organisation*, New York, Free Press.

Fook, J. (1996) 'The Reflective Researcher: Developing a Reflective Approach to Practice', in Fook. J. (ed.), *The Reflective Researcher – Social Workers' Theories of Practice Research*, St Leonards, NSW, Allen and Unwin.

Fook, J. (2002) *Socail Work: Critical Theory and Practice*, London, Sage.

Fook, J., Ryan, M. and Hawkin, L. (2002) *Professional Expertise: Practice, Theory and Education for Working in Uncertainty*, London, Whiting and Birch.

Forester, J. (1980) 'Critical Theory and Planning Practice', *Journal of the American Planning Association*, Vol. 46, No. 3, July: 275-285.

Forester, J. (1991) 'Anticipating Implementation: Reflective and Normative Practices in Policy Analysis and Planning', in D.A. Schön (ed.), *The Reflective Turn: Case Studies In and On Educational Practice*, New York, Teachers College, Columbia University.

Fransella, F. and Bannister, D. (1977) *A Manual for Repertory Grid Technique*, Academic Press, London-New York.

Freire, P. (1972) *Pedagogy of the Oppressed*, London, Penguin.

Freire, P. (1973) *Education for Critical Consciousness*, New York, Seabury Press.

Freire, P. (1996) *Pedagogy of Hope: Reliving Pedagogy of the Oppressed*, New York, Continuum Publishing Company.

Glazer, N. (1974) 'Schools of the Minor Professions', *Minerva*, Vol. XII, No. 3: 346-364.

Gleed, S. (1996) 'A First Attempt at Research: Surveying Rural Social Work Practice', in Fook, J. (ed.), *The Reflective Researcher – Social Workers' Theories of Practice Research*, St Leonards, NSW, Allen and Unwin.

Goode, W.J. (1969) 'The Theoretical Limits of Professionalization', in A. Etzioni (ed.), *The Semi-Professions and Their Organization*, New York, The Free Press.

Gould, N. (1989) 'Reflective Learning for Social Work Practice', *Social Work Education*, Vol. 8, No. 2: 9-19.

Gould, N. (1991) 'An Evaluation of Repertory Grid Technique in Social Work Education', *Social Work Education*, Vol. 10, No. 2: 38-49.

Gould, N. (1996a) 'Introduction: Social Work Education and the "Crisis Of The Professions"', in N. Gould. and I. Taylor (eds), *Reflective Learning for Social Work*. Aldershot, Arena.

Gould, N. (1996b) 'Using Imagery in Reflective Learning', in N. Gould. and I. Taylor (eds), *Reflective Learning for Social Work*, Aldershot, Arena.

Gould, N. and Taylor, I. (eds) (1996) *Reflective Learning for Social Work*, Aldershot, Arena.

Gowdy (1994) 'From Technical Rationality to Participating Consciousness', *Social Work*, Vol. 34, No. 4: 362-370.

Greenwood, J. (1998) 'The Role of Reflection in Single and Double Loop Learning', *Journal of Advanced Nursing*, Vol. 27: 1048-1053.

Habermas, J. (1971) *Knowledge and Human Interest*, Boston, Beacon Press. [First published as *Erkenntnis und Interesse*, Frankfurt, Suhrkamp.]

Habermas, J. (1974) *Theory and Practice* [translated by John Viertel], London, Heinemann.

Habermas, J. (1984) *Theory of Communicative Action*, Boston, Beacon Press. [First published as *Theorie des Kommunikativen Handelns*, 2 Vols, Frankfurt, Suhrkamp 1981.]

Harri-Augustine, S. and Thomas, L.F. (1991) *Learning Conversations: The Self-Organised Learning Way to Personal and Organisational Growth*, London and New York, Routledge.

Hartman, A. and Laird, J. (1983) *Family Centered Social Work Practice*, New York, The Free Press.

Heaney, T.W. and Horton, A.I. (1990) 'Reflective Engagement in Social Change', in J. Mezirow and Associates, *Fostering Critical Reflection in Adulthood: A Guide to Transformative and Emancipatory Learning*, San Francisco, Jossey-Bass.

Hemmens, G.C. (1980) 'Introduction: New Directions in Planning Theory', *Journal of the American Planning Association*, Vol. 46, No. 3: 259-260.

Henkel, M. (1995) 'Conceptions of Knowledge and Social Work Education', in M. Yellowly and M. Henkel (eds), *Learning and Teaching in Social Work*, London, Jessica Kingsley Publishers.

Horton, M. (1990) *The Long Haul: An Autobiography*, New York, Doubleday.

House of Commons (1879) *Report and Minutes of Evidence Poor Law Union and Lunacy Inquiry (Ireland)*, H.C. 1878-79 (2239) xxxi.

Ixer, G. (1999) 'There's No Such Thing As Reflection', *British Journal of Social Work*, Vol. 29: 513-527.

Jarvis, P. (1987) *Adult Learning in the Social Context*, London, Croom Helm.

Jarvis, P. (1992) 'Reflective Practice and Nursing', *Nurse Education Today*, Vol. 12: 174-181.

Jennings, C. and Kennedy, E. (eds) (1996) *The Reflective Professional in Education Psychological Perspectives on Changing Contexts*, London, Jessica Kingsley.

Kelly, G.A. (1955) *The Psychology of Personal Constructs*, New York, Norton.

Kelly, G.A. (1965) 'The Strategy of Psychological Research', *The Bulletin of the British Psychological Society*, Vol. 18: 1-15.

Kelly, G.A. (1969) *Clinical Psychology and Personality: The Selected Papers of George Kelly*, New York, Chichester, Wiley.

Kemmis, S. and McTaggart, R. (1982) *The Action Research Planner*, Victoria, Deakin University.

Kolb, D.A. (1974) *Experiential Learning*, Englewood Cliffs N.J., Prentice Hall.

Kolb, D.A. and Fry, R. (1975) 'Towards an Applied Theory of Experiential Learning', in Cooper, C.L. (ed.), *Theories of Group Processes*, London, John Wiley and Sons.

Labouvie-Vief, G. and Blanchard-Fields, F. (1984) 'Cognitive Ageing and Psychological Growth', *Ageing and Society*, Vol. 2, Part 2, Cambridge, Cambridge University Press.

Lanzara, G.F. (1991) 'Shifting Stories: Learning from a Reflective Experiment in a Design Process', in D.A. Schön (ed.), *The Reflective Turn: Case Studies In and On Educational Practice*, New York, Teachers College, Columbia University.

Lewin, K. (1946) 'Action Research and Minority Problems', *Journal of Social Issues*, Vol. 2: 34-46.

McGoldrick, M. and Gerson, R. (1985) *Genograms in Family Situations*, New York, W.W. Norton and Co.

McNiff, J. (1994) *Action Research: Principles and Practice*, London, Routledge.

Mezirow, J. (1981) 'A Critical Theory of Adult Learning and Education', *Adult Education*, Vol. 32: 3-24.

Mezirow, J. (1990a) 'How Critical Reflection Triggers Transformative Learning', in J. Mezirow and Associates, *Fostering Critical Reflection in Adulthood: A Guide to transformative and Emancipatory Learning*, San Francisco, Jossey-Bass.

Mezirow, J. (1990b) 'Conclusion: Towards Transformative Learning and Emancipatory Education', in J. Mezirow and Associates, *Fostering Critical Reflection in Adulthood: A Guide to Transformative and Emancipatory Learning*, San Francisco, Jossey-Bass.

Mezirow, J. (1991) *Transformative Dimensions of Adult Learning*, San Francisco, Jossey-Bass.

Mezirow, J. (1995) 'Adult Education and Empowerment for Individual and Community Development', in B. Connolly, T. Fleming, D. McCormack and A. Ryan (eds), *Radical Learning for Liberation*, Maynooth, Co Kildare, Maynooth Adult and Community Education Occasional Series No. I.

Mezirow, J. and Associates (1990) *Fostering Critical Reflection in Adulthood: A Guide to Transformative and Emancipatory Learning*, San Francisco, Jossey-Bass.

Ming Tang, N. (1998) 'Re-examining Reflection – a Common Issue of Professional Concern in Social Work, Teacher and Nursing Education', *Journal of Interprofessional Care*, Vol. 12, No. 1: 21-32.

Moroney, R.M. (1986) *Shared Responsibility: Families and Social Policy*, Hawthorn, New York, Aldine.

Newberg, N. (1991) 'Bridging the Gap: An Organizational Inquiry into an Urban School System', in D.A. Schön (ed.), *The Reflective Turn: Case Studies In and On Educational Practice*, New York, Teachers College, Columbia University.

Papell, C. and Skolnik, L. (1992) 'The Reflective Practitioner: A Contemporary Paradigm's Relevance for Social Work Education', *Journal of Social Work Education*, Vol. 28, No. 1: 18-25.

Peterson, D.R. (1995) 'The Reflective Educator', *American Psychologist*, Vol. 50, No. 12: 975-983.

Polanyi, M. (1967) *The Tacit Dimension*, New York, Doubleday.

Powell, J.H. (1989) 'The Reflective Practitioner in Nursing', *Journal of Advanced Nursing*, Vol. 14: 824-832.

Pray, J.E. (1991) 'Respecting the Uniqueness of the Individual: Social Work Practice with a Reflective Model', *Social Work*, Vol. 36: 80-85.

Putnam, R.W. (1991) 'Recipes and Reflective Learning: "What Would Prevent You From Saying It That Way?"', in D.A. Schön (ed.), *The Reflective Turn: Case Studies In and On Educational Practice*, New York, Teachers College, Columbia University.

Quinn, A. (1999) 'The Use of Experiential Learning to Help Social Work Students Assess their Attitudes Towards Practice with Older People', *Social Work Education*, Vol. 18, No. 2: 171-182.

Redmond, B. (1996) *Listening to Parents – The Aspirations, Expectations and Anxieties of Parents about their Teenagers with Learning Disability*, Dublin, Family Studies Centre, University College Dublin.

Redmond, B. (1997) 'Family Services – Power or Patronage?', *Irish Social Worker*, 15 (4), pp. 4-5.

Redmond, B. (2000) *Working Reflectively with Clients: A new teaching and learning model for professional training in the area of learning disability*, unpublished PhD Thesis, University College Dublin.

Redmond, B. (forthcoming) 'Parents and Professionals – exploring a complex relationship', in P.N. Walsh and H. Gash (eds) *Lives in Times: Perspectives of People with Disabilities*, Dublin, Wellword Publishers.

Reed, J. and Procter, S. (1993) *Nurse Education: A Reflective Approach*, London, Edward Arnold.

Reece-Jones, P. (1995) 'Hindsight Bias in Reflective Practice: An Empirical Investigation', *Journal of Advanced Nursing*, Vol. 21: 783-788.

Rivage-Seul, M. and Rivage-Seul, M. (1994) 'Critical Thought and Moral Imagination: Peace Education in Freirean Perspective', in P.L. McLaren and C. Lankshear (eds), *Politics of Liberation: Paths from Freire*, London, Routledge.

Russell, T. and Munby, H. (1991) 'Reframing: the Role of Experience in Developing Teachers' Professional Knowledge', in D.A. Schön (ed.), *The Reflective Turn: Case Studies In and On Educational Practice*, New York, Teachers College, Columbia University.

Ryan, M. (1996) 'Doing Longitudinal Research: A Personal Reflection', in J. Fook (ed.), *The Reflective Researcher – Social Workers' Theories of Practice Research*, St Leonards, NSW, Allen and Unwin.

Sadique, D. (1996) 'Undertaking the Challenge: Using Qualitative Methods to Identify Social Work Competencies', in J. Fook (ed.), *The Reflective Researcher – Social Workers' Theories of Practice Research*, St Leonards, NSW, Allen and Unwin.

Schön, D.A. (1971) *Beyond the Stable State*, New York, Random House.

Schön, D.A. (1983) *The Reflective Practitioner – How Professionals Think in Action*, New York, Basic Books.

Schön, D.A. (1987) *Educating the Reflective Practitioner: Toward a New Design for Teaching and Learning in the Professions*, San Francisco, Jossey-Bass.

Schön, D.A. (1991) *The Reflective Turn: Case Studies In and On Educational Practice*, New York, Teachers College, Columbia University.

Schön, D.A. (1992) 'The Crisis of Professional Knowledge and the Pursuit of an Epistemology of Practice', *Journal of Interprofessional Care*, Vol. 6, No. 1: 49-63.

Schön, D.A. (1995) 'The New Scholarship Requires a New Epistemology', *Change: The Magazine of Higher Learning*, Vol. 27, No. 6: 26-39.

Schön, D.A. and Bamberger, J. (1991) 'Learning as a Reflective Conversation with Materials', in F. Steier (ed.), *Research and Reflexivity*, London, Sage.

Schön, D.A. and Rein, M. (1995) *Frame Reflection: Towards the Resolution of Intractable Policy Controversies*, New York, Basic Books.

Smyth, W.J. (1992) 'Teachers' Work and the Politics of Reflection', *American Educational Research Journal*, Vol. 29, No. 2: 267-300.

Susman, G.I. and Evered R.D. (1978) 'An Assessment of the Scientific Methods of Action Research', *Administrative Science Quarterly*, Vol. 23: 582-603.

Taylor, I. (1996) 'Facilitating Reflective Learning', in N. Gould and I. Taylor (eds), *Reflective Learning for Social Work*, Aldershot, Arena.

Taylor, I. (1997) *Developing Learning in Professional Education: Partnerships for Practice*, Buckingham, SRHE and Open University Press.

Taylor, I., Thomas, J. and Sage, H. (1999) 'Portfolios for Learning and Assessment: Laying the Foundations for Continuing Professional Education', *Social Work Education*, Vol. 8, No. 2: 147-160.

Tsuin-Chen, O. (1970) 'Dewey's Lectures and Influence in China', in J.A. Boydston (ed.), *Guide to the Works of John Dewey*, Carbondale, Southern Illinois University Press.

Weiler, K. (1994) 'Freire and a Feminist Pedagogy of Difference', in P.L. McLaren and C. Lankshear (eds), *Politics of Liberation – Paths from Freire*, London, Routledge.

Winter, R. (1996) 'Some Principles and Procedures for the Conduct of Action Research', in O. Zuber-Skerrit (ed.), *New Directions in Action Research*, London, Falmer Press.

Yelloly, M. and Henkel, M. (eds) (1995) *Learning and Teaching in Social Work*, London, Jessica Kingsley.

Zeichner, K.M. and Liston, D.P. (1996) *Reflective Teaching: An Introduction*, New Jersey, Lawrence Erlbaum Associates Inc.

Zuber-Skerritt, O. (1992) *Action Research in Higher Education*, London, Kogan Page.

Index